AMERICAN LITERATURE
and
CHRISTIAN DOCTRINE

American Literature

Literature

&

Christian

Doctrine

By RANDALL STEWART

LOUISIANA STATE UNIVERSITY PRESS
Baton Rouge

TO CLEONE

Mistress of herself
though china fall

* *Preface*

THIS LITTLE treatise makes no pretense to completeness or authoritativeness. It aspires at most to an exploration, tentative and fragmentary, of a large and neglected area. I should be happy if it should prove to be the cause, or occasion, of the writing, by way of agreement and disagreement, of treatments much more complete, authoritative, and satisfactory both for the scholar and the general reader.

Since I am a teacher of American literature, I approach the subject of literature and religion from the literary side; which means, among other things, that my preparation is unequal, being much less in theology than in literature. This inequality being what it is, I find myself a bit astonished at my temerity, and some of my readers may be a bit astonished, also. If it were morally allowable, but it is not, I should blame some of my theological friends, who were so indiscreet as to endorse a little pamphlet of mine, published as a "Faculty Paper" of the Episcopal Council, in the autumn of 1955. Several of my theological friends not only expressed an interest, rather surprising to me, in this pamphlet, but went on to applaud the "soundness" of my theology. Such "soundness" as there was, I had to confess, was owing to instinct, largely, and to early training. (My father was a Baptist preacher in Tennessee.) I have said that the treatment is incomplete. I have left out many writers whom a comprehensive treatment would have to include. But I aimed from the beginning at a short, exploratory book, and I have selected the writers who interested me most, and served my partisan purpose best.

For this treatise is quite frankly partisan. I have, for the nonce, abandoned the so-highly-prized, the so-strenuously-inculcated academic neutrality. While I doubt if a professor of American literature should be quite so partisan in the classroom as I have been in this treatise, I must confess to a growing impatience with the traditional academic adoration of the objective, disinterested, neutral approach to all questions. I could name (but I won't) a thick, standard book on the history of American culture (exhaustive, scholarly) which is so neutral that it is perfectly colorless. There is an uncomfortably close kinship, I fear, between neutrality (*neutral* is related etymologically to *neuter*) and sterility.

Professors of literature have been more neutral than most, especially where moral and religious questions have been concerned. The reasons for this have been at least three: (1) professors of literature, being congenitally polite, have not wanted to step on anybody's toes; (2) they have striven (mistakenly, I think) to be as objective and disinterested as their scientific brethren; and (3) they have prided themselves (again mistakenly, I think) on their agnosticism in religious matters, agnosticism being, or having been in the past, almost universally regarded in academic circles as more scholarly, more intelligent, and more sophisticated than "belief." A shift away from this attitude is now noticeable in our college faculties and on our campuses, and I should be happy to have even a small part in helping the shift along.

I believe that there has been a good deal of confusion on the questions raised in this book, and I should be glad to clarify, if I could, the issues a little. I have insisted upon certain tests of Christian orthodoxy—the chief test being a recognition of Original Sin—and I have tried to make it

clear that while certain great writers meet these tests sufficiently to be called "orthodox," others—and among them,
some of our most famous, influential, and "democratic"
writers—have unmistakably strayed beyond the bounds of
Christian orthodoxy.

The distinction, I believe, is a useful one. It has a bearing, for one thing, on the interpretation of our culture. It
would be ironical indeed from the Christian standpoint if
the unorthodox writers were regarded as more "American" or more "democratic" than the orthodox, and yet
some of our most important historians have implied as
much, and have led us to believe that our democratic culture can be defined best in terms of the ideas of such heter-
odox thinkers as Jefferson, Emerson, and Whitman. It has
seemed to follow that democracy and Christianity are somehow incompatible.

I should be happy if this study should have the effect of
encouraging abler and better equipped investigators than
I to re-examine the bases of our democratic assumptions,
and especially to explore the needs of the present and
future. For may it not very well be that certain writers,
however important their contributions in the past, have
lost in modern times much of their usefulness, and certain
other writers, however disvalued by social historians in the
past, are about to acquire a special, new usefulness?

One of our outstanding political leaders has recently
singled out a dictum of Emerson's that "the highest revelation is that God is in every man," as expressing the true
spirit of our democracy. The following pages will argue,
among other things, not only that Emerson's deification
of man is heretical from the standpoint of Christian doctrine, but that it offers, in the long run, an unsatisfactory
rationale for the democratic way of life.

What is a Christian? And what is a democrat? For my
part, I should hope that it is possible for a man to be both
a good democrat and a good Christian without precipitat-

ing within himself a civil war. But whatever the answers to questions like these, I venture the opinion that if our democracy is to survive and thrive, it will be necessary that a genuine Christian humility (of which we seem to have scarcely any at the present time) become an essential part of our consciousness, it will be necessary that our thinking about democracy develop in a more distinctly Christian direction.

R. S.

Vanderbilt University
Nashville, Tennessee
January, 1958

✷ *Acknowledgments*

CERTAIN parts of this book have been previously printed. A part of Chapter III appeared in *Tennessee Studies in Literature* (Number 2, 1957); a part of Chapter IV appeared in *The Tragic Vision and the Christian Faith* (ed. Nathan A. Scott, Jr., Association Press, 1957); and Chapter V appeared substantially in its present form in *The Virginia Quarterly Review* (Winter, 1958). Grateful acknowledgment is given for permission to reprint these portions here.

✶ Contents

xiii

AMERICAN LITERATURE
and
CHRISTIAN DOCTRINE

I ✳ *The Fierce Faith Undying*

WHEN THE Pilgrims landed at Plymouth Rock, to quote William Bradford, "they fell upon their knees and blessed the God of Heaven, who had brought them over the vast and furious ocean, and delivered them from the perils and miseries thereof, again to set their feet on the firm and stable earth, their proper element." The style of this passage, incidentally, with its repetition and parallelism, shows that its author knew the Bible; and it is a point worth making early in any treatment, however brief, of American literature and Christian doctrine that the Bible has been the greatest single influence on our literature.

Our writers, almost without exception, have been steeped in Biblical imagery, phrasing, rhythms. This has been true of the "unorthodox" writers as well as the "orthodox," and it would be an unfortunate time for our literature if this should ever cease to be true. It is reassuring, in this connection, that one of the chief writers of our time, Robert Penn Warren, has advised young writers to read their Bible, and mark it well. Warren's writings show that he has read and marked his own Bible to good purpose.

"They fell upon their knees and blessed the God of

Heaven." That was a fine moment in our history, and Bradford, in his *History of Plymouth Plantation,* has given us a fine account of it. The Pilgrims got New England off to a good start.

This chapter deals, for the most part, with Puritanism, which we generally associate with New England. This is natural, since some of the chief exemplars of American Puritanism resided in New England in colonial times. But it is important to remember that there was Puritanism in old England as well as New England, and that American Puritanism has not been confined to colonial New England. Puritanism has cut across nations and regions, periods and sects. It has been one of the most pervasive of all influences in American life, and the term itself is so many-faceted that definition becomes difficult, if not impossible. The term, in fact, has many meanings.

To many people Puritanism means hostility to fun. This meaning is at least as old as Shakespeare's *Twelfth Night,* where Maria calls Malvolio (the name is Latin for "ill-wisher") "a kind of Puritan," and Sir Toby rebukes him in these words, "Dost thou think because thou art virtuous, there shall be no more cakes and ale?" It was perhaps owing in part to Shakespearean influence that the Prohibitionists of the 1920's were called "Puritans," and H.L. Mencken penned his famous definition of Puritanism as "the haunting fear that someone, somewhere, may be happy." This view of the matter can find a good deal of support in American history, an early instance being the cutting down of Thomas Morton's maypole at Merrymount (near Plymouth, Massachusetts) by John Endicott, a staunch "puritan," in the 1630's, and the dispersal of the "revelers." Nathaniel Hawthorne made this incident the subject of a charming tale, which, while deprecating the bigotry of Endicott, and betraying a certain nostalgia for the carefree times of Merry England, nevertheless in the resolution (where a fictional work's "intention" is especially to be

4

looked for) takes a clear, firm stand for the importance of moral earnestness. Some historians have thought (not without reason) that a good deal was at stake that summer evening at Merrymount, and the outcome of the affair meant, symbolically, that we were to become a nation incapable of true gaiety.

The Puritans stood historically for simplicity of worship. ✓ In the early seventeenth century they wanted to "purify" the English Church, rid it, that is, of ceremonies and trappings which smacked of Rome. They came into conflict with Archbishop Laud, who was very high church. They broke away from the English Church and became dissenters. Many of them migrated to Massachusetts, and helped to establish a great tradition of dissent in America.

It was this tradition which Edmund Burke in his speech on "Conciliation" with the American colonies characterized so admirably (and admiringly) as "the dissidence of dissent and the protestantism of the protestant religion." Some of the great landmarks in American literature have been landmarks in this tradition of dissent. As illustrations, consider four titles, one from each of the four centuries of American history: *The Bloudy Tenent of Persecution for Cause of Conscience* (1644) by Roger Williams; *The Declaration of Independence* (1776) by Thomas Jefferson; *Civil Disobedience* (1849) by Henry David Thoreau; and *I'll Take My Stand* (1930) by "Twelve Southerners." The naming of these titles is meant merely to suggest the vitality of a tradition whose importance in the American experience cannot be overstated. At a time like the present, when the dissenting spirit is seriously threatened by totalitarian pressures, it is well to remember that if we should lose this spirit, we should cease to be what we have been, and should become something a great deal less.

Architecturally, the "purity" of worship which Puritanism stood for embodied itself in the New England meeting

5

house. The New England meeting house is lovely to look at, with its white spire rising above the tree tops. But the box pews are uncomfortable to sit in, and the order of worship, at least in the old days, had no frills. The total effect, from one viewpoint, is very stark, very bare. The Anglican Church preferred the Gothic chapel, and the two styles have tended to divide the new world practice between them. Each style has its own merits. The spic-and-span white meeting house, which requires a fresh coat of paint annually to keep it so, doubtless had a certain appropriateness in a new society. But the Gothic chapel also has flourished in America, and wherever one finds it, it stands, among other things, for the American nostalgia for Europe, and the old Catholic ways.

√   Viewed from the economic standpoint, Puritanism in America has sometimes stressed the importance of financial success. The Bible promises "prosperity" to the righteous man ("Whatsoever he doeth shall prosper"), and some Puritans have been known to interpret material prosperity as a sign of God's special approval. Vernon Parrington was probably right in his censure of Sam Sewall on the score of his materialism. One finds a similar criterion among some Protestant sects, even today, where the rich man in the congregation is singled out as a special example of God's favor. Such a view of the Christian life and its meaning is one of the less lovely as well as less intelligent aspects of the Puritan inheritance. It is, moreover, one of the sadder commentaries on our materialistic culture that the Biblical word "prosper" should be so widely construed among us in an almost exclusively pecuniary sense.

√   Viewed in still another aspect, the moral aspect, Puritanism connotes a certain strictness, a conscientiousness. One phrase for it is "the New England conscience," which is acceptable enough if one understands that the New England conscience is not confined to New England. Matthew Arnold made a useful distinction in his essay, "Hebraism

6

and Hellenism." "Hellenism" he defined as "spontaneity of consciousness," and "Hebraism" as "strictness of conscience." Hebraism, in this contrast, can stand roughly for Puritanism.

Some have supposed that this particular aspect of Puritanism has had a bad effect on the mental health of the nation. It may be so. One hears that the real trouble with many psychiatric patients is that, afflicted with an active conscience, they have made the mistake of undertaking an immoral course—involving, perhaps, adultery, or embezzlement—for which they are unsuited by temperament and training. Walt Whitman definitely felt that we should be better off if we could rid ourselves of our guilt sense. "I think I could turn and live with animals," he exclaimed in "Song of Myself."

I think I could turn and live with animals, they're so placid and
    self-contained,
I stand and look at them long and long.
They do not sweat and whine about their condition,
They do not lie awake in the dark and weep for their sins,
They do not make me sick discussing their duty to God. . . .
Not one is respectable or unhappy over the whole earth.

Conscientiousness, of course, can be refined to the point of morbidity. *Mens sana in corpore sano* ought not to be lost sight of; it is a Christian as well as a pagan concept; St. Paul, for example, has something to say about the importance of a "sound mind." But Whitman's recommendation of reversion to the animals is not the answer to human unhappiness, because we are not animals. What will we have? Shall we trade scrupulousness for unscrupulousness? Shall we exchange decent behavior for wantonness? Problems of this sort are part of the price we pay for being human.

Theologically (to glance at one other facet of the many-faceted subject of this chapter), Puritanism is often iden-

7

tified with Calvinism, but this is not entirely correct. Edwards, to be sure, was a Calvinist. But his New England predecessors were not complete Calvinists. The old "covenant theology" of New England did not stress predestination as much as Calvin did. Samuel Eliot Morison summed up the covenant theology in this pithy fashion: "God, I've done my part, now You do Yours!" The similarity between this and Poor Richard's "God helps those who help themselves" is a bit astonishing. It suggests the tie-in (already spoken of) between Puritanism and materialism, and also helps explain Ben Franklin's admiration for Cotton Mather. Both were men of good works. But good works won't save you, according to Calvin. Only God's grace will do that.

Jonathan Edwards is not only the greatest of all American theologians (and philosophers as well), but the greatest of all American writers before the nineteenth century. Such logic, such clarity, such ordonnance (to use a word which T.S. Eliot applied to the sermons of Lancelot Andrewes) are rarely met with in American writing, or in any writing. There is severity, strictness, inexorableness, in Edwards. There are also a love of beauty, a homeliness of illustration, a tenderness, a recognition of the importance of the feelings (which Edwards liked to call the "affections") in the religious experience. There is that rare literary and philosophical (as well as personal) virtue—a balance of head and heart.

Edwards is known chiefly for his fire-and-brimstone sermon, *Sinners in the Hands of an Angry God* (1741), and anthologists who have persisted in reprinting this to the exclusion of everything else by him have done his reputation a considerable disservice. It is not my intention to minimize the importance of *Sinners in the Hands of an Angry God*. Edwards wrote it, delivered it with great effectiveness, and meant every word of it: men *are* sinners, and God *is* angry with them for their sins, and *does*

8

threaten them with dire punishment.[1] But it is well to note that Edwards' gospel is not confined to the admonitory and the punitive. And it is well to redress the balance by calling attention to another side, a more engaging side, of which his sermon *A Divine and Supernatural Light* (1734) is an excellent example.

What is this divine and supernatural light? The preacher clears the ground by specifying a few things which it is *not*.

(1) It is not "those convictions that natural men may have of their sin and misery." ("Natural" in Edwards means unregenerate; man is depraved by nature. The romantics of the nineteenth century will have a quarrel with the Calvinists on this score.) (2) "This spiritual and divine light does not consist in any impression made upon the imagination." (Notice the distrustful, deprecatory use of "imagination," a word which the romantics will rehabilitate.) (3) "This spiritual light is not the suggesting of any new truths or propositions not contained in the word of God." (Edwards here sets up a safeguard against heretical innovations by enthusiasts or fanatics. The Bible, he insists, is the supreme and final authority in matters spiritual. Emerson was later to reject such a safeguard, condemn the "stationariness" of religion, call for "a new revelation.")

Having thus cleared the ground, Edwards proceeds with a positive description. The divine and supernatural light is, he says, "a true sense of the divine excellency of the things revealed in the Word of God, and a conviction of the truth and reality of them, thence arising." He insists

[1] All of this is, in a certain profound sense, as applicable now as then. After all, is there anything in Edwards' sermon more frightening than that extraordinary picturization of an atomic holocaust, *A Short Vision*, by Peter and Joan Foldes (see *Time*, June 11, 1956)? Indeed, Edwards' sermon and *A Short Vision* have at least this much in common: they both exhibit with a good deal of theatrical effectiveness man's sin and folly, and the precariousness of his position in the universe.

9

that religion is more than a "rational" or "speculative" knowledge or belief. (The deists a little later would attempt to confine religion to the rational or speculative.) "He that is spiritually enlightened," Edwards declared, ". . . does not merely rationally believe that God is glorious, but he has a sense of the gloriousness of God in his heart. There is not only a rational belief that God is holy, and that holiness is a good thing, but there is a sense of the loveliness of God's holiness. There is not only a speculative judging that God is gracious, but a sense of how amiable God is upon that account, or a sense of the beauty of this divine attribute." Edwards then supports his argument with a homely illustration: "There is a difference [he says] between having a rational judgment that honey is sweet, and having a sense of its sweetness. A man may have the former, that knows not how honey tastes; but a man cannot have the latter unless he has an idea of the taste of honey in his mind." The key word in these passages is "sense," but it is a spiritual, not a physical sense that is meant. The physical sense of taste is used here merely by analogy. Edwards is not a "sensationalist" (as the psychologists would say) after the manner of Locke; he is a transcendentalist, albeit an un-Emersonian one.

"This evidence," Edwards continues, "that they that are spiritually enlightened have of the truth of the things of religion, is a kind of intuitive and immediate evidence. They believe the doctrines of God's word to be divine, because they see divinity in them; i.e., they see a divine and transcendent and most evidently distinguishing glory in them; such a glory as, if clearly seen, does not leave room to doubt of their being of God, and not of man."

"They that are spiritually enlightened"—how apt the phrase! And how inadequate is mere "speculation" to produce the kind of enlightenment Edwards is talking about! The famous eighteenth-century "Enlightenment" was a rational affair; but Edwards' enlightenment is "intuitive,"

"immediate," "transcendent." Emerson was to make much
of these same qualities: Emersonian Transcendentalism
was to be defined as "the intuitive perception of truth."
But it is important to note that while Emerson and Edwards would be in substantial agreement in their rejection
of eighteenth-century rationalism, the individual intuition
under Emerson is given *carte blanche,* while under Edwards it operates within well-defined limits and according
to strict rules.

The complete sovereignty of God is never in question
with Edwards, nor the complete authority of the Christian
Scriptures. The divine and supernatural light, Edwards
declares, "is immediately given by God, and not obtained
by natural means." And he goes on to explain, still further,
how this light works: "The notions that are the subject
matter of this light are conveyed to the mind by the Word
of God; but that due sense of the heart, wherein this light
formally consists, is immediately by the Spirit of God.
As for instance, that notion that there is a Christ, and that
Christ is holy and gracious, is conveyed to the mind by the
Word of God; but the sense of the excellency of Christ by
reason of that holiness and grace, is nevertheless immediately the work of the Holy Spirit." Edwards' sermon is
the finest statement I know, of the experiential nature of
religion.

I have already said that Edwards was a Calvinist. Parrington called him the last American Calvinist, and Morison
called him the first. It is possible that he was both the last
and the first, in the sense that he was the most complete
of all American Calvinists. But Calvinism was not an
anachronism in the eighteenth century, as Parrington said
it was; neither is it an anachronism today. There were Calvinists (more or less complete) before Edwards, and there
have been many since. Calvin's "Five Points" have a certain relevancy to the human condition at any time, and
this relevancy is rediscovered from age to age.

One does not have to read the three stout volumes of Calvin's *Institutes of Christianity* to find out what the Five Points are. They have been so current in American usage as to be listed (under "Calvinism") in almost all the dictionaries. I quote from *Webster's New Collegiate Dictionary: "Calvinism.* The doctrines of the French theologian John Calvin (1509–1564), including election or predestination, limited atonement, total depravity, irresistibility of grace, and the perseverance of the saints. Calvinism especially emphasizes the sovereignty of God in the bestowal of grace. Cf. Arminian." And under *Arminian,* I quote again from *Webster's:* "Of or pertaining to James Arminius (1560–1609), a Dutch protestant against the tenets of strict Calvinism. The theology of the Wesleyans of Great Britain and the Methodists of America is Arminian."

Calvinism and Arminianism, I suppose, very nearly divided the theology of the American Protestant world between them. I can recall the lively debates in Tennessee in my boyhood days between the Methodists and the Baptists. The Methodists put less stress on predestination and the irresistibility of grace, allowed a larger apparent freedom to the individual, leaned to the view that the atonement was made for all, balked at *total* depravity, and were of the opinion that saints *might* fall from grace. The Arminian theology was the more "liberal," the Calvinistic the more absolute, the more heroic, the more sublime. The difference between man and God is greater in Calvin, the position taken is more uncompromising, the view of the human condition is, I believe, closer to the fact.

The Arminians were more disturbed than the Calvinists by the apparent contradiction between the sovereignty of God and the responsibility of man. The Calvinists, indeed, were not disturbed at all, and rightly so, for there can be no contradiction between the finite and the infinite. God's predestinating providence operates in infinity; man's moral responsibility, in the limited sphere of his finite, mundane existence. The fact that the All-Wise Being makes His own ultimate disposition of events does not in the least relieve the individual person of his obligation to do his utmost toward the shaping of those events. It becomes equally important, at the same time, of course, that, having done his utmost, he bow before the ultimate disposition of the All-Wise. This tension between effort and acceptance, responsibility and acquiescence, is a central paradox of the Christian faith.

As a matter of taste in terminology, I prefer "providence" to "determinism" in speaking of the Calvinistic idea of predestination. "Determinism" is a modern scientific word, and does not involve the supernatural at all. There are various kinds of determinism—climatic, environmental, economic, biological, and the like. These determinisms play a large part (as I shall attempt to show in a later chapter) in forming the modern concept of naturalism, and do, in effect, tend to absolve the individual of responsibility, exculpate him from his wrongdoing. And therein lies the insidiousness of the naturalistic philosophy. But no such exculpation resides in the doctrine of divine foreknowledge. Moreover, it is an interesting fact of history that people who have held strongly to the doctrine of divine predestination have never been apathetic or irresponsible (as some adherents of the modern determinism seem in danger of becoming). Rather, they have taken hold of the successful alternative, as if to say, "I am 'fated' to succeed; I am predestined to victory; for if God be for us, who can be against us!" There is a vast difference, in short, between these two kinds of "determinism," which are sometimes mistakenly spoken of as if they were similar, and presented the same kind of problem. The modern determinism is generally regarded as pessimistic. There is nothing pessimistic (though some modern misinterpreters have supposed that there is) about the Calvinistic doctrine of predestination. The former implies defeat by material forces. The latter calls confidently to its aid the forces of the Almighty Himself.

If canonization were a Protestant practice, Edwards would be our first Protestant American saint. He was unsullied by the materialisms sometimes associated with Puritanism in America. He was the least worldly of men. He is our grand prototype, our best example, of the intellectual-spiritual man. Although his fame has always been considerable in academic circles, he deserves a wider reading and a closer acquaintance among the Christian laity. It is true that the Calvinistic doctrines meet with resistance in some quarters (though the resistance is probably less, in these neo-orthodox times, than formerly), but it is well to remember that Edwards' basic doctrines are, after all, the basic Christian doctrines.

In our preoccupation with particular variations among the sects, it is easy to lose sight of the broad area of general agreement. For there *is* a broad area of general agreement, there *is* such a thing as Christian orthodoxy, and in the present state of the world, the distinguishing of individual differences may be less important than the definition of orthodox essentials. Whether one's standpoint is Calvinist or Arminian, Puritan or non-Puritan, Protestant, Anglican, or Catholic, there are the following basic assumptions: (1) the sovereignty of God (God is infinitely wise, powerful, loving, and just, and is truly sovereign in His world); (2) the divinity of Christ (Jesus is the only begotten Son of God); (3) Original Sin (the natural man is imperfect, fallible, prone to evil); (4) the atonement (natural man is redeemed through faith in the efficacy of Christ's atoning death); (5) the inspiration of the Scriptures (the Bible is God's revealed Word). Surely these doctrines, broadly considered, constitute an unimpeachable Christian orthodoxy. Teachers of American literature have often had the experience of hearing their students impugn certain of these doctrines as found, for example, in Edwards, without the awareness of their being generally held throughout Christendom. Such is the theological ignorance of this secular age.

The crucial question concerns the nature of man. A good deal depends on whether man is regarded as good or bad by nature; a child of God though fallen, or the soulless product of mechanical forces; infinitely perfectible through education, or radically imperfect and therefore inescapably human; a rational being capable of saving himself through his own unaided reason, or a being whose reason, though useful and necessary, is insufficient in itself to his full and highest needs. These are questions which concern what is sometimes called the human condition, and it is one of the purposes of this discussion to explore these questions in relation to some of the chief American authors.

Mr. V.S. Pritchett, the distinguished British critic, has contributed to the *New York Times Book Review* a leading article entitled "Two Great American Puritans." Some readers of this excellent piece were doubtless amused and surprised to find that Mr. Pritchett's two great American Puritans are none other than Henry James and T.S. Eliot. It was interesting to see these writers called American, because some Americans have questioned our right to claim them—expatriates both, and naturalized British subjects. (It *was* reassuring to know that we could claim them by the leave of the British themselves.) And it was no doubt surprising to some to see these writers—cosmopolites, searchers after the older European culture, the older, richer traditions, whether in society or literature or religion— called by the "narrow," "New England" name of "Puritan."

If Nathaniel Hawthorne were being considered, there would be no question, for he was unquestionably a Puritan, or a kind of Puritan. He doubtless inherited his Puritanism from the "steeple-crowned progenitors" of the

eenth century—from William Hathorne, who or-
the whipping of the Quaker woman, naked from the
up, and John Hathorne, who, with Sam Sewall and
____m Stoughton, ordered the deaths of the Salem
witches in 1692. Hawthorne was very critical of the
bigotry, intolerance, and cruelty of the old Puritans, but
his stories usually had a way of taking the Puritan side.
Georgiana in "The Birthmark" had a blemish—the badge
of her humanity—which could not be removed without
causing her death. The adulterous lovers in *The Scarlet
Letter* were not allowed to be happy, they were not permitted to escape into a world of amoral freedom. One
recalls H.L. Mencken's definition, previously quoted—
"the haunting fear that someone, somewhere may be
happy." One recalls it, that is, if one is inclined to make a
joke about a serious matter. Yes, Hawthorne was a Puritan, perhaps the Puritan of Puritans among the great
American writers.

And then one recalls (to recur to Mr. Pritchett's pair of
authors) F.O. Matthiessen's habit of linking together the
three—Hawthorne, James, Eliot—in that most stimulating of all books ever written about American literature,
American Renaissance. For in the section on Hawthorne
in *American Renaissance,* Matthiessen, over and over
again, after having begun with a facet of Hawthorne,
moves inevitably to a comparable facet of James, and then
of Eliot. This threefold relationship, indeed, is the author's
chief pattern, and remembering this fact, one surmises
that Mr. Pritchett must be right, that James and Eliot
must be Puritans, too. And if this be true, then Puritanism has exercised a controlling influence over three of our
greatest writers.

Although these writers will be considered in some detail
in later chapters, it may be well to ask here, In what sense
or senses is the term "Puritan" applicable to the three? It
is a question which can be answered in many different ways,

16

but there is in all three a vein of asceticism, of restraint, of discipline. There is the assumption of human imperfection and of the long discipline necessary to human improvement. Words like "optimism" and "pessimism" are irrelevant in such a context. There is a point in the exploration of these writers where Puritanism and Classicism become rival claimants, or perhaps complementary tendencies, and the Puritan-Christian discipline merges with the Classic. At such a point, one is tempted to call Hawthorne, James, and Eliot Christian humanists, and be done with labeling.

Human imperfection, human improvement, the nature and purpose of the human experience—these are the crucial matters. Of works like *The Scarlet Letter, The Ambassadors, Little Gidding,* this much can be said by way of suggesting a broad basis of "Puritan" agreement: that their authors believe that the grand aim of human experience is, in the words of the old hymn, "thy dross to consume, thy gold to refine." But the word "Puritan" in this context has taken on a considerably larger connotation than it had at the beginning of our discussion. It has, in fact, usurped the legitimate role of "Christian."

The influence of Puritanism in American life and letters has been pervasive indeed. The works of the three imaginative writers whom I have called Puritan were of course, among other things, a criticism of Puritanism, that is, a critical examination, a careful weighing, of its merits and defects. The Puritan spirit is shown sometimes to be bigoted, narrow, repressive, as when John Endicott in a fit of overrighteous rage chopped down the Maypole at Merrymount. Lambert Strether (of *The Ambassadors*), the greatest of James's heroes and a quite admirable character, is a product of a Puritan culture, and his limitations (his reluctance to "enjoy," for example) reflect a Puritan asceticism. The reader is pleased to see that Strether's capacity for enjoyment has been increased somewhat at the end, thanks to the fine educative influence of that most charming of European ladies, Madame de Vionnet. Strether's education, after all, was, as James would say, very much "an affair of the senses," and the senses, the sensuous senses, had been starved in Woollett, Massachusetts, Strether's home town. Possibly the withdrawal of Eliot's Prufrock, his hopeless self-involvement, were the result of Puritan repressiveness. But despite their awareness of Puritan liabilities, these authors—Hawthorne, James, and Eliot—cannot be called anti-Puritan. Their moral earnestness stamps them indelibly and forever with the Puritan stamp.

Are not the active foes of Puritanism, too, stamped with the Puritan stamp? Many of them, I think, are. They, too, are incapable of indifference, or carefreeness, or nonchalance. Mencken attacked Puritanism with Puritan vigor and forthrightness. Carlyle said that "Socrates was terribly at ease in Zion," Socrates being quite un-Puritan in his whole attitude. But the American foes of Puritanism (I take Mencken as the best example) were never very much at ease. They, too, took seriously the Hebraic text, "Woe to them that are at ease in Zion." The strenuousness of all concerned, in fact, suggests the applicability of the adjective Puritan to our culture as a whole.

I recur once more to Arnold's suggestive essay "Hebraism and Hellenism," where Hebraism is defined as "strictness of conscience" (Happy are they who keep the law, who do the will of the Lord), and Hellenism as "spontaneity of consciousness" (Happy are they who think "justly," that is, with exactness, "rightness"). Arnold took England and America as modern examples of Hebraism, and France as an example of Hellenism. The French have long been famous for their enjoyment of the pleasures of the intellect, the free play of the mind, intellectual disinterestedness, curiosity, sheer academicism. There has never been much Hellenism, in Arnold's sense, in America. We are as a people incapable of "entertaining" rival hypotheses, of viewing matters disinterestedly for the sheer enjoyment of balancing opinions; we are poor equilibrists. Our pejorative use of the adjective "academic," as when we dismiss impatiently (even in college halls) a question which has been raised, by saying that it has "merely an academic interest," shows beyond much doubt on which side of Arnold's fence we belong. When Strether went to Paris, he was astonished at the brightness of the conversation in the circle of his young friend Chad Newsome, the number of subjects discussed, the variety of opinions expressed. It was all so different from the dogmatic, pragmatic talk to which he had been accustomed in America. But every virtue has its vice, and every vice its virtue. Perhaps today we Americans can with some complacency point to France—paralyzed and ineffectual as she is, or appears to be—as an example of the unfortunate *political* results of too much intellectual disinterestedness.

The term Puritanism still seems to attach itself more naturally and more tenaciously to New England than to any of the other regions. But the term is much wider in its application, if for no other reason than that the New Englanders have moved into other regions, especially the Middle West. The Puritanism of the other regions, however, does not necessarily stem from New England. In the South, where the "Cavalier" tradition was at first dominant, there were "Puritans" at an early date. Some of these were of Scotch or Scotch-Irish descent. Some were descendants of the old Covenanters themselves. Then, too, there were the German Lutherans, the reformed Dutch, and the Huguenots. In Virginia the Tidewater was prevailingly Anglican, the Valley, Presbyterian. West of the mountains, in Kentucky and Tennessee, in the early years of the nineteenth century, one found, besides Episcopalians and Presbyterians, the more evangelical, camp-meeting Methodists, Baptists, and Campbellites. All of these denominations, except the Episcopal, could be termed Protestant and, in certain senses, Puritan.

If the term "liberal" can be taken as an antonym to "Puritan," then the South and New England developed, paradoxically, in opposite directions: the latter, having begun in Massachusetts with Puritan strictness, became in the nineteenth century a stronghold of liberalism; while the former, having begun in Virginia and South Carolina with the amenities of the Anglican establishment, became under the decisive impact of the evangelical sects, the stronghold of fundamentalism. In the present century the South has continued conservative, and at midcentury (in the 1950's) it is the most conservative of all the American regions in almost all departments of life and thought.

There is a state of tension in the South today between the old and the new, the traditional and the antitraditional, and out of this tension (the like of which one finds nowhere else in present-day America) has come a great literary flowering, the greatest which our country has seen since the New England flowering of a century ago. It is interesting to note that the writers of this flowering are not reformers; theirs is not a literature of protest. Rather, as Donald Davidson has pointed out, it is a literature of acceptance.[2] The fictions of Faulkner and Warren, for example, like the fictions of Hawthorne and Melville, are descriptive, not reformist.

There runs through much of the writing of the Southern Revival a characteristic which Ellen Glasgow, in her fine novel of the Shenandoah, has called a "vein of iron." It is a characteristic which one associates with the old Covenanters, or with the best of the New England worthies (with Edwards, for example), or with Stonewall Jackson. This vein of iron is hard, intransigent, steadfastly loyal. Perhaps the best contemporary Southern writer to illustrate the

[2] "Why the Modern South Has A Great Literature," *Still Rebels, Still Yankees* (Baton Rouge, 1957).

quality I mean (it is definitely a Puritan quality) is Davidson, and perhaps the best poem to cite as an illustration is
his "Lee in the Mountains."

In 1865 Robert E. Lee returned to civil life and accepted
the presidency of Washington College (later to be renamed
Washington and Lee) located in Lexington, Virginia, in
the Shenandoah Valley—a region formerly associated particularly with Jackson, and now with Lee as well as Jackson. Davidson's poem is a contemplative monologue, near
the end of which Lee addresses the young men of the college as follows:

> Young men, the God of your fathers is a just
> And merciful God Who in this blood once shed
> On your green altars measures out all days,
> And measures out the grace
> Whereby alone we live;
> And in His might He waits
> Brooding within the certitude of time,
> To bring this lost forsaken valor
> And the fierce faith undying
> And the love quenchless
> To flower among the hills to which we cleave,
> To fruit upon the mountains whither we flee,
> Never forsaking, never denying,
> His children and His children's children forever
> Unto all generations of the faithful heart.

It is indicative of the persistence of the Puritan influence
to find it functioning so strongly in our two great literary
revivals—the flowering of New England a century ago, and
the renascence of the modern South. If the Puritan "center" has moved from New England to the South, the
literary evidence would seem to show (New England having been for a long while relatively sterile) that New England's loss has been the South's gain.

II   ✳   *The Great Mechanic*

Puritanism is not "irrational." Indeed, the Puritans insisted upon the reasonableness of their doctrines. But the term "rationalism," as it is applied to the "Enlightenment," which flourished, particularly, in the eighteenth century, suggests a reliance upon the rational faculty which goes far beyond orthodox Puritan, or Christian, practice, for the rationalism of the Enlightenment assumes that man can know the truth through his own unaided reason. The Puritans exercised the rational faculty within the metes and bounds prescribed by Christian doctrine; they reasoned from premises supplied by God's revealed Word; and given the premises, the conclusions were likely to be inescapable. The eighteenth-century rationalists, however, rejected these very premises, and proceeding from scratch, set up, by means of the reason alone, their entire body of doctrine.

The eighteenth-century rationalists sometimes went under the name of deists. The deists were not a church; they had no ecclesiastical organization; there is probably no way of knowing how many people in a given time and place regarded themselves as deists. The movement (it was a kind of philosophical movement) reached its apogee in the last quarter of the eighteenth century. It cannot be said ever to have been very popular, or to have taken a very strong hold in America. But its prestige was great at the time of the formation of our government, especially because leaders like Paine, Franklin, and Jefferson were of the deistic persuasion. Moreover, the deistic influence was a far-reaching one. It was quite noticeable in Unitarianism, which in turn made itself felt later among the "liberal" membership of many Protestant sects.

Some of the best-known hymns which we sing in church today have deistic overtones. The most famous of these is one by Joseph Addison, which goes, some of my readers will recall, as follows:

> The spacious firmament on high
> With all the blue etherial sky
> And spangled heavens, a shining flame,
> Their great Original proclaim.
> Th' unwearied Sun from day to day
> Does his Creator's power display;
> And publishes to every land
> The work of an Almighty hand.
>
> Soon as the evening shades prevail,
> The Moon takes up the wondrous tale;
> And nightly to the listening Earth
> Repeats the story of her birth:
> Whilst all the stars that round her burn,
> And all the planets in their turn,
> Confirm the tidings as they roll,
> And spread the truth from pole to pole.
>
> What though in solemn silence all
> Move round the dark terrestrial ball;
> What though nor real voice nor sound
> Amidst their radiant orbs be found?
> In Reason's ear they all rejoice,
> And utter forth a glorious voice;
> For ever singing as they shine,
> "The Hand that made us is divine."

Nearly a hundred years later Tom Paine was to write in his *The Age of Reason* (1795) a prose version of the same argument. Yet Addison, who was a good Anglican, would not have agreed with Paine's disavowal of the Christian scriptures. Although both pointed to the Nineteenth Psalm ("The heavens declare the glory of God, and the firmament sheweth His handiwork") as sufficient authority for their respective compositions, the difference (it is an important one) between Addison and Paine is that whereas Paine found in the "heavens" the entire basis of his deistic religion, Addison would see *there* only a corroboration of a more primary source, namely, the Christian revelation. And so it is misleading (and historically and biographically inaccurate) to call Addison's hymn "deistic," though to a modern reader it sounds that way. The modern deist finds it, I imagine, a congenial and fairly complete statement of the religious question.

The key word of the eighteenth century both in England and America, the word most frequently used in the writings of that era, is "reason." "In Reason's ear," said Addison, capitalizing "Reason," and the eighteenth century quite appropriately came to be called by Paine's title, "The Age of Reason." The French revolutionists attempted (unsuccessfully) to set up in Notre Dame, instead of the old Catholic worship, the worship of the Goddess of Reason.

The rationalists believed man to be a rational creature, and many people cherished a new confidence in the availability and efficacy of man's reason. The masses of men, Jefferson believed, could be depended upon to act in a rational manner. It is sometimes said that this new faith in man's rationality was a necessary basis for the great democratic movements of the century—the revolutions in America and in France. It may be so, but it is worth noting that, actually, the two revolutions gave only a partial support to the new faith. The American revolution was conducted rationally enough for the most part, but the revolution in France soon became hysterically irrational. Edmund Burke (that great neglected political writer, who, as John Morley once said, "treated politics with thought and imagination") was not guilty of the inconsistency sometimes charged against him when he supported the one, and deprecated the other.

The greatest writer of the century, Jonathan Swift, in his greatest book, *Gulliver's Travels,* can hardly be said to have shared the century's confidence in man's rationality. He was, on the contrary, at some pains to show man's proneness to irrational behavior (as, for example, in his accounts of the controversy between the Big-Endians and the Little-Endians, and the performances and successes of the political acrobats). The rational creatures in the book were not men, but horses, and while Gulliver rightly preferred the Houyhnhnms to the Yahoos, he does not seem to have profited much by their instruction, for at the end of the story Gulliver himself is guilty of the most irrational act of the entire book when he deserts his family (who are not Yahoos) and goes to live with a horse (who is not a Houyhnhnm). Moreover, the social evenings among the Houyhnhnms were certainly very dull affairs, and it is difficult to believe that the brilliant Dean Swift, author of the *Journal to Stella,* and lover of wit and gossip, could be seriously recommending such society. The book seems to say not only that man is prone to irrationality but that pure rationality, even if it were attainable, would make the world a less interesting place.

Two of the great American rationalists, Paine and Jefferson, lacked Swift's witty and wise perception of men and events. They were great public servants, but they were solemn and humorless. Only solemn, humorless men, I fear, would be capable of putting such unlimited confidence in "reason." They lacked, too, the modern understanding of the schizophrenic roles of intellect and emotion in the unintegrated person, to whom the irrationality of his emotionally compulsive acts is perfectly clear.

Paine's *Age of Reason* is the classic statement of American deism. The author says, "The natural bent of my mind was to science." In his opinion, "It would be advantageous to the state of learning to abolish the study of the dead languages, and to make learning consist . . . in scientific knowledge." He rejects the revelation of the Christian Bible as mere "hearsay." "It is a contradiction in terms and ideas," he reasons, "to call anything a revelation that comes to us at second-hand, either verbally or in writing." He discusses the doctrine of the virgin birth in language which has seemed irreverent to many readers:

When also I am told that a woman called the Virgin Mary, said, or gave out, that she was with child without any cohabitation with a man, and that her betrothed husband, Joseph, said that an angel told him so, I have a right to believe them or not; such a circumstance required a much stronger evidence than their bare word for it; but we have not even this—for neither Joseph nor Mary wrote any such matter themselves; it is only reported by others that *they said so*—it is hearsay upon hearsay, and I do not choose to rest my belief upon such evidence.

This is clearheaded and hard-hitting. But many readers are likely to be less impressed by the argument than by Paine's lack of historical imagination. One recalls a very different treatment of the Virgin Mary in the *Mont-Saint-Michel and Chartres* of Henry Adams, who, himself an intellectual man, had at once (what Paine so egregiously lacked) a historian's and a poet's sense of the past. The Virgin, Adams beautifully showed, was the beneficent intermediary between the human and the divine. The worship of the Virgin built the great cathedrals; it culminated artistically in the Rose Window at Chartres. Adams, New

England intellectual that he was, became himself almost her worshiper, he was almost persuaded. "If you had only the soul of a shrimp," he despairingly cried, "you would crawl . . . to kiss her feet." But worshiper or not, Adams the historian saw in the Virgin the symbol of infinite energy—the mediaeval symbol, which he contrasted so alarmingly with his modern symbol, the dynamo. "Mediaeval man," he said, "was the servant of the Church; modern man is the servant of the Power House." The mediaeval age, Adams thought, was one of "unity." The modern age, he added, is one of "multiplicity"—a multiplicity which he was to spell out in the *Education*.

Vernon Parrington professed to wonder at the odium in which Paine was held in America: "a strange reward," he said, "for a life spent in the service of mankind." But there was nothing very strange about it. Paine, I'm afraid, was impervious to the whole realm of spiritual and aesthetic values. He did more than disagree with certain religious beliefs. In his blunt, unimaginative way, he outraged the religious and poetic sensibilities of the Christian world.

Paine proposed to substitute the "Creation" for the Christian Bible: "Some perhaps will say— Are we to have no word of God—no revelation? I answer Yes; there is a word of God; there is a revelation. *The word of God is the creation we behold.* And it is in this word, which no human invention can counterfeit or alter, that God speaketh universally to man."

Paine's Bible, then, is the "creation." This creation is a machine (a most ingenious machine), and the Creator is a "great mechanic." His theology is the study of "the structure and machinery of the universe," "the geometry of the universe," and his church is "a school of science." One can't help feeling that Paine's God, the great mechanic (whose existence is established as a necessary inference from the existence of the machine), is not very immediately or passionately interested in his creation. He has presuma-

bly gone off about other business, for the machine is perfect, or nearly so, and requires little, if any, tinkering.

The whole philosophy is cold and impersonal, it seems
to me. The trouble with Paine's system is that even though
man may live in a mechanical world (which appears doubtful), man himself is not a machine, and he cannot worship
a God who is nothing more than a mechanic. Mechanical
marvels are all very well, but they cannot satisfy man's
inner needs. Man's needs transcend the mechanical, they
go beyond the power of a mechanic to satisfy. His deepest
needs are, in fact, spiritual.

The following lines of the 116th Psalm present a very
different, and a more satisfying, view of the nature of God
and of man's relation to Him (they also touch us more
deeply than the Nineteenth Psalm, already referred to):

> I love the Lord because he hath heard my voice
> and my supplications. Because he hath inclined his
> ear unto me, therefore will I call upon him as
> long as I live. The sorrows of death compassed
> me, and the pains of hell gat hold upon me: I
> found trouble and sorrow. Then I called upon the
> name of the Lord: O Lord, I beseech thee, deliver my soul.
> Gracious is the Lord, and righteous; yea, our Lord
> is merciful. The Lord preserveth the simple;
> I was brought low, and he helped me. Return unto
> thy rest, O my soul, for the Lord hath dealt
> bountifully with thee. For thou hast delivered my
> soul from death, mine eyes from tears, and my feet
> from falling.

The inappropriateness of addressing such words to Paine's
"great mechanic" is obvious enough. Melville once remarked to Hawthorne that the reason why, in his opinion,
so many men distrust, and at bottom, "hate God," is that
they fancy him "all brain, like a watch." It was obviously
a deistic God like Paine's whom Melville was describing.

Jefferson's concept of God was probably less coldly mechanical than Paine's, but his confidence in man's all-sufficient reason was quite as great. In a letter to Peter Carr, one of his favorite nephews, dated Paris, August 10, 1787, Jefferson remarked under the heading of "Religion":

Your reason is now mature enough to examine the subject of religion. . . . Fix reason firmly in her seat, and call to her tribunal every fact, every opinion. Question with boldness even the existence of a god; because, if there be one, he must more approve of the homage of reason, than that of blindfolded fear. . . . Read the bible, then, as you would read Tacitus or Livy. . . . Those facts in the bible which contradict the laws of nature must be examined with care. . . . For example, in the book of Joshua we are told the sun stood still for several hours. . . . You are astronomer enough to know how contrary it is to the law of nature that a body revolving on its axis as the earth does, should have stopped, should not by that sudden stoppage have prostrated animals, trees, buildings, and should after a certain time have resumed its revolution, and that without a second general prostration. . . . Keep your reason firmly on the watch. . . . Your own reason is the only oracle given you by heaven.

Even after a large allowance is made for the influence of the age (for can not, must not, a great man transcend his age?), the modern reader, taught to look for symbolic truth, cannot help feeling a certain disappointment in Jefferson's literal-mindedness; his concern with mere historicity, mere factual, "scientific" accuracy; his unawareness of symbolic meanings; his reading of a spiritual book as if it were a historical treatise; his supposition that spiritual values must rest indispensably upon the historicity of the narrative; his assumption that the "truth" of religion and the "truth" of history are necessarily one and the same; his ignorance, in short, of the truth of "myth." It is an error which the scientist or the historian sometimes makes even today, but one which the student of literature has learned better than to make. How much nearer the "truth" (the spiritual, personal truth, which is the only kind of truth one need be concerned with in religion as well as litera- ture) Tennyson was in the opening lines of *In Memoriam:*

> Strong Son of God, immortal love,
> Whom we, that have not seen thy face,
> By faith, and faith alone, embrace,
> Believing where we cannot prove. . . .

Religion without faith, without believing where we can- not prove, is scarcely religion at all.

Franklin was more tolerant than Paine, more genial than Jefferson. His emphasis upon reason, though, his large reliance upon the rational faculty, puts him side by side with them in the deistic camp. Like Jefferson, he "fixed reason firmly in her seat, and called to her tribunal every fact, every opinion."

An interesting example of Franklin's use of "reason" in dealing with a question which is essentially one of religious faith is found in a letter to George Whatley dated Passy, May 23, 1785, where he offers the following argument for belief in the immortality of the soul:

When I observe that there is great frugality, as well as wisdom in his works, since he has been evidently sparing both of labor and materials; for by the various wonderful inventions of propagation, he has provided for the continual peopling of his world with plants and animals, without being at the trouble of repeated new creations; and by the natural reduc- tion of compound substances to their original elements, capa- ble of being employed in new compositions, he has prevented the necessity of creating new matter; so that the Earth, Water, Air, and perhaps Fire, which being compounded from Wood, do, when the Wood is dissolved, return, and again become Air, Earth, Fire, and Water; I say, that, when I see nothing an- nihilated, and not even a drop of Water wasted, I cannot suspect the annihilation of souls, or believe, that he will suffer the daily waste of millions of minds ready made that now exist, and put himself to the continual trouble of making new ones. Thus finding myself to exist in the world, I believe I shall, in some shape or other, always exist.

This is, of course, an argument from analogy, and an interesting one. Franklin appeals to the scientific principle known as the conservation of matter to give reasonableness to an analogous spiritual principle, which might be called the conservation of souls (or the conservation of personalities). Like all arguments from analogy, it does not establish certainty. At best, it only sets up an a priori likelihood. It is an argument which interests, especially, the modern scientific age, and one meets with it from time to time in the writings of scientists who are interested in religious questions.

But it is important to note that Franklin's argument is not a Christian approach to the question of the immortality of the soul. The Christian belief is based upon faith, and that faith is based upon faith in the resurrection of Jesus, and His promise of everlasting life to all believers. The Christian believer does not require scientific or quasi-scientific arguments with which to buttress and supplement the words of Jesus: "I am the resurrection and the life. He that believeth in me, though he were dead, yet shall he live. And whosoever liveth and believeth in me shall never die."

Franklin was the most tolerant of all the great Americans. It was not at all necessary that a deist be a fiery blasphemer like Paine. On the contrary, we associate deism in America more especially with tolerance and reasonableness—the gracious tolerance and the sweet reasonableness of a Franklin, or a Jefferson. I like the tone of graciousness and courtesy in the following passage from a letter which Jefferson wrote to Miles King from Monticello, September 26, 1814:

I must ever believe that religion substantially good which produces an honest life, and we have been authorized by One whom you and I equally respect, to judge the tree by its fruit. Our particular principles of religion are a subject of accountability to our God alone. I inquire after no man's, and trouble none with mine; nor is it given to us in this life to know whether yours or mine, our friend's or our foe's, is exactly the right one. Nay, we have heard it said that there is not a Quaker or a Baptist, a Presbyterian or an Episcopalian, a Catholic or a Protestant, in heaven; that, on entering that gate, we leave those badges of schisms behind, and find ourselves united in those principles only in which God has united us all. Let us not be uneasy, then, about the different roads we may pursue, as believing them the shortest, to that our last abode; but, following the guidance of a good conscience, let us be happy in the hope that by these different paths we shall all meet in the end. And that you and I may there meet and embrace, is my earnest prayer.

This is very fine. Equally fine as an example of tact and tolerance—and perhaps more famous—is Franklin's letter, written only a few weeks before his death, to a Calvinistic theologian, President Ezra Stiles of Yale, who had enquired concerning his religious beliefs. "You desire to know something of my religion," Franklin began, and continued as follows:

It is the first time I have been questioned about it. But I cannot take your curiosity amiss, and shall endeavor in a few words to gratify it. Here is my creed. I believe in one God, Creator of the universe. That He governs it by His Providence. That He ought to be worshipped. That the most acceptable service we render Him is doing good to His other children. That the soul of man is immortal, and will be treated with justice in another life respecting its conduct in this. These I take to be the fundamental principles of all sound religion, and I regard them as you do in whatever sect I meet with them.

As to Jesus of Nazareth, my opinion of whom you particularly desire, I think the system of morals and his religion, as he left them to us, the best the world ever saw or is likely to see; but I apprehend it has received various corrupt changes, and I have, with most of the present Dissenters in England, some doubts as to his divinity; though it is a question I do not dogmatize upon, having never studied it, and think it needless to busy myself with it now, when I expect soon an opportunity of knowing the truth with less trouble. I see no harm, however, in its being believed, if that belief has the good consequence, as probably it has, of making his doctrines more respected and better observed; especially as I do not perceive that the Supreme Being takes it amiss, by distinguishing the unbelievers in His government of the world with any peculiar mark of His displeasure.[1]

I shall only add, respecting myself, that, having experienced the goodness of that Being in conducting me prosperously through a long life, I have no doubt of its continuance in the next, without the smallest conceit of meriting it. . . . I confide that you will not expose me to censure and criticism by publishing any part of this communication to you. I have ever let others enjoy their religious sentiments, without reflecting on them for those that appeared to me unsupportable and even absurd. All sects here [in Philadelphia], and we have a great variety, have experienced my good will in assisting them with subscriptions for building their new places of worship; and, as I never opposed any of their doctrines, I hope to go out of the world in peace with them all.

Carl Van Doren calls this letter "the tolerant words of a great pagan skeptic." The words are indeed tolerant, and it is fortunate that tolerant men like Franklin and Jefferson presided over the formation of our government. Had it not been so, those basic principles of religious freedom, and separation of Church and State, might not have been so solidly imbedded in our Constitution. But I should like to insist at this point that it does not follow from the fact that some of our chief founders were not orthodox Chris-

[1] This last clause is a good example of spiritual imperviousness.

tians—it does not follow, as some have supposed, that ortho-dox Christianity offers no basis for a rationale of democ-racy. This is a question, and an important one, I think, to which I should like to recur in a later chapter.

Franklin, the greatest of the rationalists, and Edwards, the greatest of the theologians; Franklin, the greatest of the utilitarians, and Edwards, the greatest of the experts in the psychology of religion; Franklin, the greatest of the diplomatists, and Edwards, the most intransigent of men—these two giants divided between them the Ameri-can eighteenth century, and they have divided America and the American mind between them ever since. Edwards could never have sat in the Constitutional Convention, for he lacked the political sagacity; Franklin could never have written "A Divine and Supernatural Light," for this child of the "Enlightenment" was spiritually unenlight-ened. Tolerance came almost too easily to Franklin, as it does to all skeptics. Edwards approached bigotry, his re-ligious convictions were so intensely felt.

A surface view of our culture would suggest that Amer-ica has followed Franklin rather than Edwards. This seems especially so when we think of the material and tech-nological aspects of our culture, for Dr. Franklin started us on the road which has led to a gadgeteers' paradise. But now that it is becoming startlingly clear that gadgets can't save us, and may all too readily destroy us; now that thoughtful members of this mechanistic age are seriously asking the question which the Philippian jailer, trembling, put to Paul and Silas, "Sirs, what must I do to be saved?"; now that Dr. Franklin's lightning rod begins to look, from one viewpoint, like a pathetic symbol of human pride and inadequacy, while Edwards' soul-probings seem more searching to this generation of readers perhaps than they have ever seemed before, it is possible that Edwards will yet emerge, is already emerging, as the more useful, the more truly helpful of the two, in man's present distress.

34

The rationalism of the eighteenth century had a greater influence on Unitarianism than on any other religious sect (deism being not a sect but a philosophy). The founder of American Unitarianism, William Ellery Channing, emphasized the rational approach to religious questions. In his famous sermon on "Unitarian Christianity" (delivered in Baltimore in 1819, at the ordination of Jared Sparks), Channing expressed confidence in man's reason in general, and particularly in its use in the interpretation of the Bible. "We profess not to know a book," he said, "which demands a more frequent exercise of reason than the Bible. . . . We feel it our bounden duty to exercise our reason upon it perpetually." Channing rejected the tenets of Calvinism because they seemed to him unreasonable.

Paine, by the same token, had rejected Christianity, bag and baggage. Now Channing, of course, was no bedfellow of Paine's. He was respectful of the Christian revelation. The Bible and Jesus to Channing were not without a certain authority. But Calvinism, he thought, was a sad perversion of the truth. God is pure benevolence, he reasoned. Jesus was the most virtuous of *men*. Man is not by nature sinful. The doctrine of the atonement is a bloody and irrational doctrine. Religious excitement is open to grave suspicion. "When," Channing said, "we observe a fervor called religious in men whose general character expresses little refinement and elevation, and whose piety seems at war with reason, we pay it little respect."

Boston Unitarianism under Channing's leadership became decorous, rational, unimpassioned, and fashionable. "Whoever clung to the older faith," Barrett Wendell once wittily remarked, "did so at his social peril." The novels of William Dean Howells (who was almost as great an expert in Boston social distinctions of the last century as John P. Marquand is, in our own age) contain pathetic, amusing examples of Wendell's "peril." I have in mind particularly Ben Halleck in *A Modern Instance,* who was

35

a Baptist, and whose maladjustment to his Boston world was aggravated both by his not having gone to Harvard (he went to a New England provincial college) and by his not being a Unitarian.

It may not be correct to charge Channing himself with complacency or pride, but he may well have been the cause of it in others. "We think it ungrateful to disparage the powers which our Creator has given us," he begins. "Men may trust their faculties too little as well as too much," he goes on, and then declares that "the ultimate reliance of a human being is and must be on his own mind." [2] Well, a number of eminent Christian writers—Milton, Bunyan, and Hawthorne among them—would demur. One would suppose that the ultimate reliance of a human being is and must be on God—as when Luther said, "God help me, I can do no other." There can be little doubt that Channing gave aid and comfort to a kind of social-intellectual complacency.

An interesting example of this complacency came under my observation not long ago when an estimable lady of mature years, whom one might with some justice call intellectual and Unitarian, declared to me privately and emphatically, after a religious meeting during which the speaker had ventured to say a good word for Original Sin, that she did not feel that she was sinful at all. She meant that she was not aware of having committed sinful acts, that her life was morally upright, that she was the chaste wife of one husband, that she was a lady and not a sinful woman. Such a view, of course, misses the point in the doctrine of Original Sin, which refers not so much to overt acts as to the whole nature of man, his limitations, his fallibility, his self-involvement, the "wrongness" of his attitudes, the absence of contrition and humility, the pres-

[2] These quotations are from another famous discourse by Channing, "The Moral Argument Against Calvinism," delivered in Boston in 1820.

ence of pride. In Christian doctrine, indeed, pride is the greatest sin, and the lady in question, far from being sinless, was unwittingly guilty of the greatest sin of all.

Emerson began under Channing's influence but before long he broke away. He began as a Unitarian minister, but after some four years, in the early 1830's, he resigned his pastorate, offering as explanation his unwillingness to administer the Lord's Supper. He said that he had lost interest in this sacrament. But probably there were other considerations. One perhaps was his aversion to the fashionableness of Unitarianism in and around Boston. And more important, probably, was the emphasis by Channing, and by Unitarians generally, upon the reliance to be placed on man's *reason*.

Channing, as we have seen, had been influenced very considerably by eighteenth-century rationalism. "Reason" is almost as much a key word with him as it is with the great deists Paine, Jefferson, and Franklin. Emerson, on the other hand, reacted with a good deal of vigor against the rationalism of the earlier age. What the Christian church needed to be revitalized, he told the Harvard ministerial candidates in his "Divinity School Address" of 1838, was "first, soul, and second, soul, and evermore, soul."

By "soul" he meant the intuitive faculty, or intuition, as opposed to the rational faculty, or reason. Reason was staid, formal, logical, earthbound, uninspired. As Transcendentalist, he urged the intuitive perception of truth, the truth which lies beyond the reach of logic and reason and the physical senses.

In his exposition of this Transcendentalist philosophy (it is important for readers of Emerson to remember), Emerson did a confusing thing, semantically: he adopted the word *Reason,* usually capitalized, to mean this same intuitive faculty, and used the word *Understanding,* usually capitalized, to mean what people ordinarily understood (and understand) by *reason*. He could cite the authority of Kant, Coleridge, and Carlyle, but the terminology has confused many readers. If Emerson thought that he could domesticate the Kantian *Reason,* and that this sense of the word would supplant the older sense in American usage, he was greatly mistaken. The Emersonian usage did not catch on at all, scarcely even among close disciples like Thoreau. But Emerson's rejection of rationalism and his doctrine of "soul" did catch on. The nineteenth century, in America as in Europe, was prevailingly antirationalistic.[3]

I return to the three great deists—Paine, Franklin, and Jefferson—with whom this chapter has been chiefly concerned. Paine has been the least popular of the three in America, despite the fact that his service to the Revolution was probably the greatest. His unpopularity, as we have seen, was owing chiefly to the uncouth expression of his religious views. These views were probably not very different from those of Jefferson and Franklin, but *they* avoided Paine's odium by being diplomatists. Franklin, we recall, requested Ezra Stiles please not to embarrass him by making public the contents of his rather frank and free letter on the subject of his religious opinions.

Of the three men, Franklin has been the most popular. Americans have not worried too much about whether or not he believed in the inspiration of the Bible, or the divinity of Christ. He has been, for one thing, the grand archetype of the "successful" American. He began at the bottom, and worked his way, resourcefully and fairly, to the top. Everybody remembers that when Franklin arrived in Philadelphia, he had just enough money to buy a loaf of bread, and that he walked down the main street munching it in broad daylight. Then, too, he struck at the very beginning the keynote of our civilization, the note of

---

[3] Emerson as romanticist, and his influence, will be considered in a later chapter.

"progress": he paved the streets, calculated the optimum draft of canal boats, founded the *Saturday Evening Post,* discovered the identity of lightning and electricity. Franklin was the true patron saint of business-minded, progressive Americans—of Americans who believe (as someone has aptly put it) that "the business of America is business." And once more, his personal charm, his tact, his benign wit, his triumphs abroad, his personal success with the aristocrats of France—these and many other traits and achievements have endeared him to his fellow Americans. Rationalist or not, skeptic or not, materialist or not, Franklin is, and will always be, one of our most honored men.

Jefferson never enjoyed a personal popularity even remotely approaching Franklin's. Moreover, his pedantries at one time attracted a good deal of petty partisan ridicule and satire. (I have in mind, particularly, Washington Irving's *Knickerbocker History* and William Cullen Bryant's juvenile composition called *The Embargo.*) But of the three men, Jefferson contributed the most important body of political philosophy, and as the years went by, he came to be regarded, irrespective of political party, as the chief founder of American democracy. His *Declaration of Independence,* his *First Inaugural,* and his *Second Inaugural* have been reprinted in all anthologies of American writing. The worship of Jefferson perhaps reached its apogee in Vernon Parrington's *Main Currents in American Thought* (three noble volumes published in 1927–1930), the chief aim of which was to establish Jeffersonism, once and for all, as the highest wisdom and the true guiding light of America's destiny.

In recent years Jeffersonism has been regarded with a more critical eye in some quarters. There have arisen a neo-conservatism in politics and a neo-orthodoxy in religion, which have been inclined to look askance at some of Jefferson's large assumptions—the assumptions, for example, that man is basically good; that he can be counted

39

on to behave rationally as a general thing; that the masses of men, if given freedom of choice, can be trusted to choose the wise and good.

A view has been gaining some acceptance, roughly since World War II, to the effect that Jefferson—noble theorist that he was, and able champion of the rights of man—was a bit naive; that he did not sufficiently take into account the passions of men, and their disposition to evil; that the natural goodness theory does not square as well with the events of history as the Calvinistic notion of natural depravity; that the "failure" of the "American Dream" (of which Jefferson was the father) was owing not so much to this or that act or event as to the outmoded (as many people had supposed) premise of Original Sin; that when you came right down to it, there was no valid reason to suppose that the New World would produce Sinless Beings, that human beings could escape the human condition by the simple expedient of setting up shop on a new continent.

The most impressive criticism of Jeffersonism in modern literature is Robert Penn Warren's book-length poem, *Brother to Dragons,* published in 1953.

The poem has to do with a brutal murder committed in 1811 in western Kentucky (on a plantation located at the point where the Cumberland River flows into the Ohio) by the two sons of Thomas Jefferson's sister. Though Jefferson never alluded to this crime, the author supposes that it must have been unbearably shocking to him to discover the enormities of which his own flesh and blood was capable, and all the more so because of the benign view of human nature which he had held, and made famous throughout the world. The fact that the murder was the hacking to pieces, with an axe in the meat-house, of a Negro slave by two white men added to the irony, for Jefferson had opposed Negro slavery and declared the equality of all men.

Warren calls the poem "a tale in verse and voices." The

interlocutors, the author says, "appear and disappear, as
their inner urgencies, and the urgencies of the argument,
swell and subside." "The place of meeting," he says, "is
'no place,' and the time is 'any time.' " The speakers—
Jefferson, his sister Lucy, Lilburn and Isham Lewis the
murderers, RPW the author, Meriwether Lewis, Jefferson's cousin and onetime secretary, who with Clark led
the famous Expedition, and the others—are disembodied
spirits. The poem resolves itself into a discussion, with illustrations, of the human condition.

A long speech by Meriwether Lewis toward the end
of the poem gives an account of the hardships of the jour-
ney through the Louisiana Territory to the Pacific Coast,
the rigors and the unlovely, unromantic aspects of the raw
natural world, and after the return of the exploring party
and Meriwether's appointment as governor of the Louisiana
Territory, the political connivance which presumably
drove him to suicide. Meriwether complains of having
been misled, and made unprepared to live in the actual
world, by Jefferson's "great lie"

> . . . that men are capable
> Of the brotherhood of justice . . .

Meriwether speaks in part, as follows:

Had I not loved and lived your lie, then I
Had not been sent unbuckled and unbraced
To find the end—Oh, the wilderness was easy!—
But to find, in the end, the tracklessness of the human heart.

The discovery came late, and I was unprepared.
You had unprepared me. I hated you. . . .
For in your lie was my death,
And if I learned anything in my earthly years,
It is that every lie is a death, for I died a death.
And especially that lie spoken in the vanity of virtue . . .
Yes, that sweet lie.
And I would honor more the axe in the meat-house,

As more honest at least, than your special lie
Concocted, though out of nobleness—oh, yes
It was noble, but was concocted for your comfort
To prove yourself nobler in man's nobleness.
Yes, in man's nobleness, you'd be the noble Jefferson.
And if that is not vanity—

Meriwether Lewis's last speech is broken off when a pained and wiser Jefferson interrupts to say:

My son, be still a moment.
If what you call my lie was what undid you,
So be it, then. It has undone me, too.
For I, too, was unprepared for the nature of the world,
And unprepared, I confess, for my own nature,
And Truth, long since, began her hideous justice,
For all lies are avenged, at last, in the truth of pain . . .

It is not easy to say to what extent Warren's poem may foreshadow a general reaction against the Jeffersonian philosophy.

III   * *The Deification of Man*

WHAT IS ROMANTICISM?[1] The answer must be that it is a number of different things. And because it is so many-faceted (it is somewhat like Puritanism in this respect), it is (again like Puritanism) one of the most difficult and confusing of terms. And yet in critical discourse (like Puritanism, once more), we can hardly get along without it.

One of the most famous definitions of romanticism is the one phrased by Theodore Watts-Dunton, friend of Swinburne, as "the renascence of wonder." The rationalistic mind of the eighteenth century seemed prosaic and unimaginative to the nineteenth century. The romantics discovered a brave new world. The romantic poet strove to see and feel. His habitual attitude was one of wonder at the mystery and beauty of all created things. Emerson described the poet as "Lover of all things alive,/ Wonderer at all he meets . . ." Walt Whitman was the greatest wonderer of all. He regarded all phenomena as miraculous: "As for me," he declared, "I know of nothing else but miracles."

---

[1] I omit from the present discussion the currently popular definition of romanticism as "the idea of organic growth" because this definition happens to fit both the "romantics" of this chapter and those whom I call, in the next chapter, "counter-romantics."

43

One of the chief characteristics of nineteenth-century romanticism was the "return to nature." And the kind of nature which interested most romantics was not the geometric Newtonian universe (which appealed so much to eighteenth-century deists like Paine) but the nature which could be apprehended immediately by the five senses. The ocean and the mountains came in for an unprecedented appreciation; and so did the little, humble things—Burns's field mouse, for example, or Emerson's rhodora. Following Wordsworth (the chief influence in this return to nature), Emerson, in the "American Scholar," expressed delight in the fact that "the near, the low, the common" were being "explored and poetized." It is significant in this connection that Whitman took "leaves of grass"—the common people of the vegetable world—as the symbol of his poetry.

There were wonderfully fresh new notes in the romantic nature poetry. One was the note of particularity, close observation, original comparison. (Consider as an example Emily Dickinson's description of a snake as "a whiplash/ Unbraiding in the sun.") Another note was a rich sensuousness. (Keats and Whitman contain the best examples of this.) And a third was a religious, or quasi-religious, sentiment. To most romantic poets, nature is beneficent, peaceful, happy. Nature comforts, restores, fortifies the troubled spirits of men. (Lanier's "Marshes of Glynn" is a good example of this office of Nature.)

At this point in the discussion, one begins to capitalize *Nature,* for Nature becomes an emanation of God. In romantic poets like Wordsworth, Emerson, Whitman, God is identified with Nature, and Nature is part and parcel of God. One worships Nature, or God-in-Nature, one is not quite sure which, for in much romantic nature poetry, Nature-worship and God-worship seem a bit confused, one with the other. The basic theological error here is the con-

44

fusion of the Creator with the Thing Created. Th
mantic poet is forever running the risk of mistaking
for a tree.

The Christian God is transcendent, and at the same time,
paradoxically, immediately present and available. He is,
without being identical with nature, "closer than breath-
ing, nearer than hands and feet," as Tennyson so happily
put it.

Trees, individually and collectively, are interesting symbols. The forest, to the early New England Puritans, was
a symbol of evil. It was a place of darkness and danger.
Witch-meetings were held there (see Hawthorne's "Young
Goodman Brown"). Indians, who were pagans and instru-
ments of the devil, lurked behind trees. Hawthorne's lovers in *The Scarlet Letter,* Arthur and Hester, mentally
re-enacted in the forest their sin (its first, physical com-
mitment probably took place there, too), and the author
says quite explicitly that the forest symbolizes "moral error," a going astray, a getting lost. (This is directly reminiscent of Edmund Spenser's "error's wood" in *The Faerie
Queene.*) To the deist, trees were a very minor part of
"the creation." If the deist thought of a tree at all, it was,
probably, as another instance of symmetry, orderliness,
law. His tree, too, would be, most likely, a generic, "ideal"
tree, not a particular one with individual peculiarities. To
the romantics, the tree was divine, or possessed attributes
of divinity, and the forest was the best place for worship.
The aisles in a forest were cathedral-like. "The woods were
God's first temples," said William Cullen Bryant in "A
Forest Hymn," and this cathedral not made with hands
was a better place for worship than any church or meeting
house.

It is only a step from the goodness and wonder of Nature to the goodness and wonder of Man (one could reason
in either direction, and in a romantic context one feels

45

disposed to capitalize *Man,* also). An important aspect of romanticism is the belief that man is innately good and infinitely perfectible.

If one asks the difference between the romantic's concept of the human condition and the deist's, the answer must be that the difference is considerable; for although both have confidence in what might be called the human capacity, the romantic's view is the more elevated. While your deist is getting along pretty well, thank you, after a pedestrian fashion, depending on his good old "reason" to save him from the quagmires, or get him out, once in, your romantic must soar into the empyrean, catch the spark from heaven, sit at the right hand of God the Father, if not on the Throne itself, and all by a kind of effortless levitation.

T.E. Hulme in his *Speculations* defined "romantics" as all those who reject the doctrine of Original Sin, and this is perhaps of all the definitions the most useful and the best. For the romantics saw Man as a sinless being surrounded by a sinless Nature. The Fall of Man, they thought, had been greatly exaggerated. In fact, there had been no Fall at all.

Emerson's "Divinity School Address" is so useful for the purposes of this discussion that I should like to go over it in some detail. It was delivered before the Senior Class of the Harvard Divinity School, Sunday evening, July 15, 1838. It is a lovely, classic utterance. How beautifully Emerson begins!

In this refulgent summer, it has been a luxury to draw the breath of life. The grass grows, the buds burst, the meadow is spotted with fire and gold in the tint of flowers. The air is full of birds, and sweet with the breath of the pine, the balm-of-Gilead, and the new hay. Night brings no gloom to the heart with its welcome shade. Through the transparent darkness the stars pour their almost spiritual rays. Man under them seems a young child, and his huge globe a toy. The cool night bathes the world as with a river, and prepares his eyes again for the crimson dawn. The mystery of nature was never displayed more happily. . . . One is constrained to respect the perfection of this world. . . .

The world, Emerson goes on to say, is but "an illustration and fable" of man himself. Since this is so, the "perfection of the world" would seem to posit man's own "perfection."

Emerson believes that we can be certain of two basic assumptions: first, that we live in a universe in which good is the true reality, and evil an unreality; and second, that man can know the truth intuitively.

The first assumption Emerson develops, in part, as follows:

Good is positive. Evil is merely privative, not absolute: it is like cold, which is the privation of heat. All evil is so much death or nonentity. Benevolence is absolute and real. So much benevolence as a man hath, so much life hath he. For all things proceed out of this same spirit, which is differently named love, justice, temperance, in its different applications, just as the ocean receives different names on the several shores which it washes. All things proceed out of the same spirit, and all things conspire with it. Whilst a man seeks good ends, he is strong by the whole strength of nature. In so far as he roves from these ends, he bereaves himself of power, of auxiliaries; his being shrinks out of all remote channels, he becomes less and less, a mote, a point, until absolute badness is absolute death.

Emerson's system, then, is a monism. There is no conflict, in the strict sense, between good and evil because evil is a mere negation, a minus quantity; no struggle between God and the Devil because the Devil is a "nonentity," that is, he does not exist.

Emerson is without doubt very helpful, in a therapeutic way, in what he says about the positive power of good, and much of the recent literature of encouragement (*The*

47

Power of Positive Thinking, and the like) stems from the passage just quoted, or similar sources. But it may be a question as to how realistic it is to deny the existence of the great Adversary of the good. Are there not times when the Evil Angel seems at least as real as the Good Angel? Is a warless world, a world without conflict and struggle, the kind of a world with which we are actually acquainted?

Emerson's second large assumption is that man *can* know the truth intuitively. Of this spiritual faculty by which one apprehends the truth, Emerson writes:

It is the beatitude of man. It makes him illimitable. Through it, the soul first knows itself. It corrects the capital mistake of the infant man, who seeks to be great by following the great, and hopes to derive advantages *from another,*—by showing the fountain of all good to be in himself, and that he, equally with every man, is an inlet into the deeps of Reason. . . . Whilst the doors of the temple stand open, night and day, before every man, and the oracles of this truth cease never, it is guarded by one stern condition; this, namely; it is an intuition. It cannot be received at second hand.

Man, then, knows the truth intuitively, and each man's private intuition is authoritative for him. The image of the "inlet" or estuary is a favorite one with Emerson. Man is a tidal stream; he has a special and immediate relation to the ocean, or "Reason," or God. His tidal reactions are in no way dependent upon the tidal reactions of other men.

Emerson's use of "Reason" (as has already been noted) is likely to mislead the uninitiated reader. Here "Reason" seems to denote what Emerson liked to call the "Over-Soul," with which the individual soul mingles, as a tidal stream mingles with the ocean into which it flows. Elsewhere, Emerson's Reason is used to name the spiritual faculty by which man apprehends God. In either case, the word has to do with spiritual reality. Emerson's "Understanding" is a lower faculty—the equivalent, roughly, of "reason" as ordinarily understood. The "Understanding" is concerned with mundane affairs, the data of the senses, the "appearances," the temporal; the "Reason," with the unseen realities, spiritual truths, the eternal. The Understanding functions by logic, demonstration, proof; the Reason, by apprehension, intuition. When Emerson spoke of "my England of the Understanding, my Germany of the Reason," he meant that England was less idealistic than Germany, and more practical. In making such a comparison he had in mind the English Utilitarian school of Bentham as contrasted with the German idealistic school of Kant.

Having dealt with the two basic assumptions that good is the only reality, and that man is capable of knowing the truth by intuition or "Reason," Emerson goes on to point out what he regards as the two cardinal errors of historical Christianity.

The first "error" is that historical Christianity, he says, "has dwelt with noxious exaggeration about the *person* of Jesus." Emerson is here objecting to the doctrine of the divinity of Christ as ordinarily understood. How did this "error" come about? Emerson offers the following explanation:

Jesus Christ belonged to the true race of prophets. He saw with open eye the mystery of the soul. Drawn by its severe harmony, ravished with its beauty, he lived in it, and had his being there. Alone in all history he estimated the greatness of man. One man was true to what is in you and me. He saw that God incarnates himself in man, and evermore goes forth anew to take possession of his World. He said, in this jubilee of sublime emotion, "I am divine. Through me, God acts; through me, speaks. Would you see God, see me; or see thee, when thou also thinkest as I now think." But what a distortion did his doctrine and memory suffer in the same, in the next, and in the following ages! There is no doctrine of the Reason which

49

will bear to be taught by the Understanding. The Understanding caught this high chant from the poet's lips, and said, in the next age, "This is Jehovah come down out of heaven. I will kill you if you say he was a man."

When Jesus, then, claimed to be divine, he did not mean, Emerson maintained, that the claim should be taken in an exclusive or peculiar sense. The difference between Jesus and ordinary mortals is, according to Emerson, one of degree rather than of kind. Emerson professed not to deny "divinity" to Christ so much as to claim "divinity" for all men (which was, of course, to deny divinity to Christ, as "divinity" is ordinarily understood). Emerson's view probably was (or at least eventually became) acceptable to the Unitarians as well as to the Transcendentalists. One recalls in this connection the fine monument of William Ellery Channing, located in Boston, at the corner of Arlington and Boylston streets, on which is inscribed the ringing pronouncement: "He breathed into theology a humane spirit, and proclaimed anew the divinity of man."

The divinity of man! Channing and Emerson elevated man to a dizzy eminence, and the historians generally have applauded the elevation. Van Wyck Brooks in *The Flowering of New England,* for example, says that "by raising the general estimate of human nature, which the old religion had despised," the new view "gave a prodigious impulse to the creative life."

One must demur with Brooks on at least two counts.

First, the old religion had "despised" (or taken a depreciatory view of) the *natural* man, but had exalted *regenerate* human nature. It had not despised human nature when once it is transformed, illumined, by the divine and supernatural light. From the Christian standpoint, the distinction between natural and regenerate, unredeemed and redeemed, is decidedly worth insisting upon.

Second, it may very well be that the revised estimate of

human nature stimulated the creative life, but the stimulation was not entirely in the direction, or of the kind, which Brooks's statement might be supposed to imply. For, as we shall see in the next chapter, the important works of the literary imagination—the fictions of Hawthorne and Melville, for example—were written not so much in agreement as dissent; they offered not so much an endorsement as a "criticism" of the revised view. Hawthorne showed in *Ethan Brand,* Melville showed in *Moby Dick,* that it may be a dangerous and terrible thing for man to usurp the role of God, to arrogate to himself "divinity." The crux of the matter is that Channing and Emerson denied the Fall of Man, and while the new view had a certain efficacy of its own, its most important result in literature was to stimulate a reaction in the opposite direction. The most important literature of the period must be regarded as a countermovement to the romanticism of Channing and Emerson.

There is no denying the popularity of the view which asserted the divinity of man. It was reassuring and cheerful. But the long-run effect was of doubtful value. In so far as it prevailed (and it prevailed more widely than readily meets the eye), there was danger of its producing complacency, bumptiousness, arrogance. It was conducive not to humility, but the opposite. To the extent that the view became a part of our national character, we became less tolerable both to ourselves and to other nations.

If the first "error" of historical Christianity—to return to Emerson's "Address"—was the exaggeration of the person of Jesus, the second was the assumption that "revelation" is finished, that the Bible is the complete and final word of God. "Men have come to speak of the revelation," says Emerson, "as somewhat long ago given and done, as if God were dead." "It is my duty to say to you," he continues, "that the need was never greater of a new revelation than now." "Tradition characterizes the preaching of this country," he objects; "it comes out of the memory, and not out

51

of the soul." We forget, he declares, "that God is, not was; speaketh, not spake." And then Emerson moves on into his eloquent, challenging peroration:

> Let me admonish you, first of all, to go alone; to refuse the good models, even those which are sacred in the imagination of men, and dare to love God without mediator or veil. Friends enough you shall find who will hold up to your emulation Wesleys and Oberlins, Saints and Prophets. Thank God for these good men, but say, "I also am a man. . . ."
>
> Yourself a newborn bard of the Holy Ghost, cast behind you all conformity, and acquaint men at first hand with Deity. . . .
>
> I look for the hour when that supreme Beauty which ravished the souls of those Eastern men, and chiefly of those Hebrews, and through their lips spoke oracles to all time, shall speak in the West also. The Hebrew and Greek scriptures contain immortal sentences, that have been bread of life to millions. But they have no epical integrity; are fragmentary; are not shown in their order to the intellect. I look for the new Teacher that shall follow so far those shining laws that he shall see them come full circle; shall see their rounding complete grace; shall see the world to be the mirror of the soul; shall see the identity of the law of gravitation with purity of heart; and shall show that the Ought, that Duty, is one thing with Science, with Beauty, and with Joy.

If the Unitarians were willing to go along, at least part of the way, with the divinity-of-man doctrine, they balked at Emerson's final point. They were not willing to accept the doctrine of unlimited revelation. There was a great protest against the "Divinity School Address," and the interesting thing about the protest is that it came more conspicuously from the Unitarians themselves than from the orthodox party. The Edwardsians could say, "We're not surprised, we're not surprised at all, at Mr. Emerson's heresies. This is the sort of thing that your Unitarianism inevitably leads to." The Unitarians were all the more an-

noyed by the taunts of the orthodox because they felt that
Emerson had betrayed their cause, had handed them over
to the enemy. Emerson was not asked back to Unitarian
Harvard to lecture for thirty years.

He *had* gone pretty far. "Thank God for these good
men!" And who, pray, were these good men? Why, the
brothers Wesley, Isaiah, Saint Paul, Jesus—good men all!
But good though they be, they are not to be regarded as
having intrinsic superiority, or any special authority, over
you and me. For I also am a man; I also am a newborn
bard of the Holy Ghost; I can make my own Bible, write
my own Scriptures. A new Bible will sooner or later come
out of the Western world which will be superior to the one
we have, for *that* is full of imperfections. The new Bible
will resolve all contradictions, reconcile all opposites. It
will show the unity, the identity of all things. It will show
Duty to be one with Science, gravitation one with purity
of heart.

Emerson elevated man to the position of deity, elim-
inated conflict, and cast over all a benign air. Science, as
we have known it, has had little to do with Duty, and the
identity of gravitation and purity of heart is not readily
visible. Emerson's monism just about erases all differences
and distinctions. It bears no recognizable resemblance to
the world and the life we know. Man is disembodied. A
millennium of pure abstraction is proclaimed. The human
condition is annulled.

"Emerson discredited more than any other man," Allen
Tate said in *Reactionary Essays* (1936), "the puritan drama
of the soul." And Tate went on to say:

The age that followed, from 1865 on, expired in a genteel
secularism, a mildly didactic order of feeling whose orna-
ments were Lowell, Longfellow, and Holmes. "After Emerson
had done his work," says Mr. Robert Penn Warren, "any
tragic possibilities in the New England culture were dis-
sipated." Hawthorne alone in his time kept pure, in the

primitive terms, the primitive vision; he brings the puritan tragedy to its climax. Man, measured by a great idea outside himself, is found wanting. But for Emerson man . . . being himself the Over-Soul, is innately perfect; there is no struggle . . . because there is no possibility of error. There is no drama in human character, because there is no tragic fault. It is not surprising, then, that after Emerson, New England literature tastes like a drink of cambric tea. Its very center of vision has disappeared. There is Hawthorne looking back, there is Emerson looking not too clearly at anything ahead. Emily Dickinson, who has in her something of them both, comes in somewhere between.

From the standpoint of the present discussion, it would be hard to improve upon Tate's statement of the case.

It is easy, of course, to be unfair to Emerson. If his "Trust thyself" was interpreted by some Americans to mean "Every man for himself," the interpretation was a perversion which Emerson himself did not foresee, and would not have endorsed, at least in the economically unscrupulous sense which we associate with the robber barons. If he denied the special authority of the Christian Scriptures, and strewed his pages with passages from non-Christian sources (especially the sacred books of the Hindoos), (1) one suspects that he liked to shock the conventionally pious hearer and reader, and (2) one notes that, after all, he made a larger use of the Christian Bible than of any other book. When he wanted to state "the first and the last lesson of religion," he could do no better than quote St. Paul's "the things that are seen are temporal, the things that are unseen are eternal." If he asserted innate goodness, and minimized evil almost to the vanishing point, he was not completely unaware of the actual existence of evil. In middle life, he became painfully aware, for example, of the evil of Negro slavery; and of the Fugitive Slave Law of 1850, he said, with unprecedented profanity, "I will not obey it, by God."

These qualifications and extenuations are true enough, and yet the fact remains that Emerson is the arch-heretic of American literature, and Emersonism the greatest heresy. By no dint of sophistry can he be brought within the Christian fold.[2] His doctrine is radically anti-Christian, and has done more than any other doctrine to undermine Christian belief in America.

I want to consider, briefly, just one other piece by Emerson, namely, "Self-Reliance." This has been over the years probably the most widely read and best-known, in America, of all American essays. Here, the author calls for, among other things, greater self-reliance in religion. He says that creeds are a disease of the intellect, and prayers a disease of the will. He has the following interesting things to say about prayer:

Prayer that craves a particular commodity, anything less than all good, is vicious. Prayer is the contemplation of the facts [3] of life from the highest point of view. It is the soliloquy of a beholding and jubilant soul. It is the spirit of God pronouncing his works good. But prayer as a means to effect a private end is meanness and theft. It supposes dualism and not

[2] Thoreau's case is interestingly different. Although he began as a disciple, or quasi-disciple, of Emerson, he was by no means a thoroughgoing Emersonian. Consider, for example, this flaming passage from "A Week," where he is talking about the New Testament: "I know of no book that has so few readers. There is none so truly strange, and heretical, and unpopular. . . . 'Seek first the kingdom of heaven.' 'Lay not up for yourselves treasures on earth.' 'If thou wilt be perfect, go and sell that which thou hast, and give to the poor, and thou shalt have treasure in heaven.' 'For what is a man profited, if he shall gain the whole world, and lose his own soul? or what shall a man give in exchange for his soul?' Think of this, Yankees. . . . They never *were* read, they never *were* heard. Let but one of these sentences be rightly read from any pulpit in the land, and there would not be left one stone of that meeting-house upon another." There is reason to believe that Thoreau's growing estrangement from Emerson was owing to his vision of evil (a vision which Emerson never had), which showed man to be truly "fallen," and in need of a radical redemption.

[3] By "facts," Emerson means spiritual reality as opposed to the data of the senses. This is another instance of his difficult vocabulary.

unity in nature and consciousness. As soon as a man is at one with God, he will not beg. . . .

The view of prayer here expressed is far removed from the Christian view. The word "soliloquy" gives the whole thing away. Prayer, to Emerson, is not man talking to God; it is man talking to himself; it is, as he says, a "soliloquy." And man is not only talking to himself, he is congratulating himself upon himself, and upon the general state of affairs. While admiration and praise are a legitimate and important part of a Christian's prayer, the admiration and praise are not properly directed to the one praying, but to God and His works. The Christian prayer recognizes the great gap which separates man from God; it is in fact based upon the very dualism which Emerson denies. The Christian prayer *does* often "beg"; it is a petition; "beseech" is one of the most frequently recurring words in all prayers of the Christian Church. Christian prayer may, and often does, quite properly crave a particular commodity: "Give us this day our daily bread," is an example.[4] Most important of all, Christian prayer has as its very basis and starting point contrition for sin, the classic instance being that of the publican, who smote his breast, and cried "God be merciful to me a sinner," and went down to his house justified.

The following prayer comes from *The Book of Common Prayer,* but it could be said, without material change, by all Christians, everywhere:

Almighty and most merciful Father, we have erred and strayed from thy ways like lost sheep. We have followed too much the devices and desires of our own hearts. We have offended against thy holy laws. We have left undone those things which we ought to have done; and we have done those

---

[4] "Bread" is, to be sure, symbolical of the spiritual bread of life, but the symbolism, to be meaningful, presupposes the material substance.

things which we ought not to have done; and there is no
health in us. But thou, O Lord, have mercy upon us, miserable
offenders. Spare thou those, O God, who confess their faults.
Restore thou those who are penitent, according to thy promises
declared unto mankind in Christ Jesus our Lord. And grant,
O most merciful Father, for his sake, that we may here-
after live a godly, righteous, and sober life, to the glory of thy
holy name. Amen.

The prayer of the miserable offender for forgiveness is
not a soliloquy of a beholding and jubilant soul.

The importance of the difference between the Christian's prayer and Emerson's cannot be overemphasized.
One says, "I am a sinner"; the other, "I am good." One
says, "God be merciful, God forgive my sins"; the other,
"My Godlike qualities are indeed reason for self-congratu-
lation." There can be no doubt, I think, that the Emerson
view, whatever our formal professions may have been, became long ago an indistinguishable and almost unconscious
part of the "American mind." It slipped in by the back
door. Just as Emerson's "Trust thyself" became (without
his intending that it should) "Every man for himself" (giving a kind of rough justice to Tate's remark, in the book
already quoted from, that Emerson became unwittingly
"the prophet of a piratical industrialism," and indeed one
recalls that Emerson's saying, "If you build a better mouse-
trap, the world will beat a path to your door," became the
golden text of our competitive economy), so his "I am
good, good innately," has suffered a whole succession of
noxious sea-changes: "I am as good as you"; "I am better
than you"; "America is good"; "America is better than any
other nation—our prosperity proves it." It is well to remind
ourselves occasionally of a text which has not been much
quoted in modern times: "Pride goeth before destruction,
and an haughty spirit before a fall."

The historians of our culture have emphasized two facts
which are especially interesting in the context of this study;

first, that our Constitution was the product of the Age of Enlightenment, when confidence in man's unaided reason was widespread; and second, that the democratic base of our society was greatly broadened during the nineteenth century, when leaders of thought like Emerson inculcated the doctrine of man's divinity. These two facts are indisputably true, and there was undoubtedly a connection in each instance between the prevailing philosophy and the political achievement: belief in man's rationality encouraged the founding fathers to set up the kind of government they did—the brilliantly reasoned structure was a crowning achievement of the Age of Reason; and confidence in man's "divinity" may very well have been a motive force back of the extension of suffrage, the emancipation of the slaves, the broadening of economic and social privileges, which characterized the nineteenth century in America. But it does not follow that the success of democracy was, or is, dependent upon "rationalism" or "romanticism," that orthodox Christian doctrine is intrinsically undemocratic, or that Christianity must be without a rationale of democracy since so many leaders in our democratic development have drawn upon doctrines of a non-Christian sort. And it does not follow, particularly, that these non-Christian doctrines are as useful now as they appear to have been in former times.

The bases of our democratic ideology need re-examination. It is no longer satisfactory to many people to interpret this ideology in terms of Paine's rationalism or Emerson's Transcendentalism. I consider myself a pretty good democrat, but I am not willing to subscribe to the views of either Paine or Emerson. I prefer to subscribe to the Christian view. But my impression is that some ideologists are reluctant to admit one into the democratic camp unless he has at least a tincture of Paine and/or Emerson. Such ideologists would do well to look around a bit. How would they fit into their scheme the fact, for example, that Hawthorne, who was a Christian and believed in Original Sin, voted for Andrew Jackson, the people's candidate, while Emerson, who was not a Christian and believed in the divinity of man, voted for John Quincy Adams, the candidate of aristocratic station and privilege? Facts like these—it would be interesting to see how many such facts one might be able to accumulate—should give one pause.

Paine and Emerson (though differing sharply between themselves) set up, each in his own way, a man-centered world. Christian doctrine sets up a God-centered world. There is a vast difference between the two. One difference, among others, is that one view leads to arrogance, and the other to humility.

It would be unfortunate indeed if those who consider themselves democrats and at the same time hold to Christian doctrine should allow themselves to be read out of the democratic faith, or should suppose that they would have to modify the Christian view, or accept non-Christian views, in order to become acceptable democrats, on the assumption that "Christian" and "democratic" are contradictory terms. If the question were looked into properly, it might be discovered that orthodox Christian doctrine offers the best rationale for democracy of all rationales, and the most useful one for these times. I refer to St. Paul's text, "All have sinned, and come short of the glory of God."

All have sinned! It is the most democratic of propositions! And it has the advantage over some other propositions of being factually and literally true; it is beyond doubt the truest of all democratic propositions. It has the further advantage of producing an attitude, a tone, a character which would recommend the democratic idea, more winningly than in the past, to a suspicious and alien world. As between the two preambles, "Let us humbly confess our sins unto Almighty God" and "Let us congratulate ourselves upon our innate goodness," the former *does* seem more favorable to a tolerable society and a viable world order.

Emerson had a great (though sometimes embarrassing) ally in the romantic camp in Walt Whitman.

Whitman sent Emerson in 1855 a copy of the first edition of *Leaves of Grass,* and received in reply one of the most famous letters ever written by one American writer to another.

I am not blind to the worth of the wonderful gift of Leaves of Grass. I find it the most extraordinary piece of wit and wisdom that America has yet contributed. I am very happy in reading it, as great power makes us happy. It meets the demand I am always making of what seems the sterile and stingy Nature, as if too much handiwork or too much lymph in the temperament were making our Western wits fat and mean. I give you joy of your free and brave thought. I have great joy in it. I find incomparable things said incomparably well, as they must be. I find the courage of treatment which so delights us, and which large perception only can inspire. I greet you at the beginning of a great career, which yet must have had a long foreground somewhere for such a start. I rubbed my eyes a little to see if this sunbeam were no illusion; but the solid sense of the book is a sober certainty. It has the best merits, namely, of fortifying and encouraging. . . .

Whitman was so pleased with the letter that he included it, without asking Emerson's permission, in the second edition of the *Leaves,* published the following year, and he printed in gold letters on the backstrip the ringing words, "I greet you at the beginning of a great career, R.W. Emerson." Emerson commented, "Walt shouldn't have done that. If I had known he was going to publish my letter, I should have enlarged the *but."* Emerson was all the more disturbed because the second edition contained the "Children of Adam" poems, whose free treatment of sex caused a good many readers (especially in and around Boston) to express surprise at Mr. Emerson's endorsement. Actually, Emerson had not seen these particular poems, and before the third edition of the *Leaves* went to press, in 1860, he tried to persuade Whitman (the two walked back and forth on Boston Common one whole morning) to omit, or at least revise, "Children of Adam." This Whitman refused to do. Emerson's admiration cooled after that. He wrote Whitman no more letters of praise, nor did he rally to Whitman's support in 1865 when Whitman lost his job in the Department of the Interior, on the strength of the accusation that he had written "an immoral book." Emerson was not always happy when his own chickens came home to roost. Perhaps he failed even to recognize them as his.

Nothing seems clearer than that Whitman was well-grounded in Emerson before he wrote *Leaves of Grass*. Not only is the thought often the same, there are many verbal echoes. Whitman, like Emerson, declared all things good, elevated the individual, deified man. I cite just one instance, though a striking one. As the narrator leans on the rail of the Brooklyn ferry (in the poem "Crossing Brooklyn Ferry") and watches in the current below his reflection and the reflections of the other passengers leaning on the rail, he sees, he says, "fine centrifugal spokes of light diverging from my head, and from each of the other heads, in the sunlit water." These spokes of light, of course, are halos. In Christian art, the halo, or "glory," is restricted to the Holy Family and to saints. Whitman confers this mark of peculiar sanctity indiscriminately upon everybody.

Whitman went beyond Emerson in certain respects. Both rejected the Five Points of Calvinism, but Emerson could not escape the Puritan inheritance, the strictness of conscience, the voice of duty, "the Ought." While Emerson was incapable of relaxation, Whitman was wonderfully relaxed: "I loaf and invite my soul," he said. There was a temperamental inner check in Emerson to counterbalance (for him, if not for others) his theoretical free-thought; he was rather an ascetic, temperamentally. Whitman was anti-Puritan, anti-innercheck, anti-ascetic. "Spontaneous me!" he cried. He celebrated the body as well as the soul, he maintained. He was the first American writer to celebrate sex.

Whitman was more "democratic" than Emerson. There are, to be sure, some good sweeping propositions in Emerson: *Every man* is directly inspired by God; *every man* is equally an inlet into the deeps of Reason; and so on. Propositions like these give us a broad enough base in theory. But Whitman is warmer, friendlier. He talks about "the love of comrades," and seems to think that this, if we can get enough of it, will make America a true democracy. He likes to hobnob with the "common" people, to "go freely [as he said] with powerful, uneducated persons." Perhaps he makes too much of a show of this camaraderie. Squeamish readers have thought that he was too affectionate, too ready (to use a favorite expression of his) to hook his arm around your waist, especially if you happen to be a man. His apparently equivocal, or dual, sexual attitude has disturbed some. But even though we may question the good taste of this demonstrativeness, there seems to be no valid reason to doubt the sincerity of his affection for all members of the human race.

Whitman's poetry is suffused with charity, and a great tenderness. His admirers have thought his charity Christlike, and indeed not without cause. Consider, for example, the passage on the prostitute in the "Song of Myself":

> The prostitute draggles her shawl, her bonnet bobs
> on her tipsy and pimpled neck.
> The crowd laugh at her blackguard oaths, the men
> jeer and wink to each other.
> Miserable! I do not laugh at your oaths nor jeer you.

These lines recall (with differences) the account of the woman taken in adultery, and particularly the words of Jesus, "He that is without sin among you, let him first cast a stone at her," and "Neither do I condemn thee." Some have called Whitman's charity a pose. It is true that he liked to think of himself as a new Messiah. But it is very wrong, I think, to dismiss him as a poseur.

Whitman stands for brotherly love, complete equality. It is his great point, and his "catalogues," which show the point best, and which have usually been disvalued, are the best things in his work. To illustrate, I quote from Section 15 of the "Song of Myself":

The pure contralto sings in the organ loft;
The carpenter dresses his plank—the tongue of his
      fore-plane whistles its wild ascending lisp;
The married and unmarried children ride home to their
      Thanksgiving dinner;
The pilot seizes the king-pin—he heaves down with a
      strong arm . . .
The farmer stops by the bars, as he walks on a First-day
      loafe, and looks at the oats and rye;
The lunatic is carried at last to the asylum a confirm'd case,
(He will never sleep any more as he did in the cot
      in his mother's bed-room;)
The jour printer with gray head and gaunt jaws works
      at his case,
He turns his quid of tobacco while his eyes blurr with
      the manuscript;
The malform'd limbs are tied to the surgeon's table,
What is removed drops horribly in a pail . . .
The young fellow drives the express-wagon—(I love him
      though I do not know him). . . .
As the woolly-pates hoe in the sugar-field, the overseer
      views them from his saddle. . . .

Form and subject here are one, and the equality is in the form. The lines are end-stopped and co-ordinate. The versification is an embodiment of the author's concept of a democratic society: the lines march shoulder to shoulder, without any taint of subordination one to another. They march with a sense at once of individual self-containment, and of being a part of a large company. The catalogues illustrate perfectly in their form the thought of Whitman's lines: "One's self I sing, a simple separate Person,/ Yet utter the word Democratic, the word En-Masse."

The democratic gospel can find much in Whitman to admire and quote. But it is as impossible to square Whitman, as Emerson, with Christian doctrine, and for the same reasons. Whitman, like Emerson, rejected Original Sin, the atonement, the special authority of the Christian Scriptures. Like Emerson, too, he blurred distinctions: between natural and regenerate, bad and good, wrong and right, low and high, inferior and superior. Everybody in Professor Whitman's class gets an A.

Now there *is* such a thing as Christian equality. It is an equality of humility: all have sinned, have erred, have strayed from Thy ways like lost sheep. And this kind of equality has the advantage of safeguarding certain radical, necessary distinctions: between good and evil, heaven and hell, salvation and damnation. For Christian doctrine recognizes, paradoxically, a hierarchical principle, a scale of values: there are thrones and dominions, principalities and powers. There is inclusion and exclusion: "Not every one that saith unto me, Lord, Lord, shall enter into the kingdom of heaven." Excellence cannot exist in a distinctionless world.

"There will soon be no more priests," Whitman announced in his famous 1855 "Preface" to the *Leaves of Grass*. And he went on to say:

Their work is done. They may wait awhile, perhaps a generation or two, dropping off by degrees. A superior breed shall take their place, the gangs of kosmos and prophets en masse shall take their place. A new order shall arise and they shall be the priests of man, and every man shall be his own priest. The churches built under their umbrage shall be the churches of men and women. Through the divinity of themselves shall the kosmos and the new breed of poets be interpreters of men and women and of all events and things. They shall find their inspiration in real objects of today. . . .

This would seem to be a complete renunciation of the Christian tradition, and indeed of all tradition. Whitman's world, as I have said before, is man-centered. The apotheosis of man has never been carried farther, nor has the apotheosis of the material present. Whitman's "real objects of today," which are to supply the inspiration for his "church" of the future, sound suspiciously like our current technological marvels.

In Whitman's vocabulary, words like "egotism" and "arrogance" are the opposite of pejoratives: they are "good words." "I dote on myself," he says in the "Song of Myself," "there is that lot of me and all so luscious." "Nothing, not God, is greater to one than one's self is/ Nor do I understand who there can be more wonderful than myself," he continues in the same vein. One understands perhaps the sense in which Whitman means all this, but it is still all very foolish and very wrong. Emerson said that Whitman had the great merit of "encouraging," but we should first enquire what it is that he encourages us to be. It would seem that he encourages us to be mighty pleased with ourselves.

I want to consider in this context, finally and briefly, two other poets, namely, Lanier and Emily Dickinson, who have been generally regarded as a part of the romanticism of their time. It is true that they are "romantic" in certain respects. But in certain other respects I think they can be separated sharply from the main romantic current of Whitman and Emerson.

Lanier's reputation as a poet has declined considerably

since 1900, and it is about time, I think, for his poetry to begin to be somewhat more highly regarded. The critical reaction against the nineteenth century pushed Lanier pretty far down the scale, and the metaphysical revival (based to a large extent upon the discovery of John Donne's virtues) helped Lanier almost not at all, for though Lanier, like the metaphysical poets, is "conceitful," his conceits have usually been pronounced bad by the new critics. And bad I suppose most of them are. But I confess to a sneaking fondness for Lanier, bad conceits and all.

Lanier's upbringing in Macon, Georgia, was strict Presbyterian, and he went to Oglethorpe, a Presbyterian college. Although he was intrigued by the various isms of his century—progressivism, scientism, liberalism, naturism, and the like—I think it very doubtful if Lanier ever abandoned the basic Christian tenets. He is perhaps one of the comparatively few American poets of stature in the nineteenth century (Dickinson is another) who can be called Christian.

His best poem is "The Marshes of Glynn," and a very interesting poem it is, despite the faults which logicians and formalists like to find in it. The action is in three parts. In the first part, the narrator has spent a long summer's day in the woods, on the Georgia coast, engaged in prayer:

Beautiful glooms, soft dusks in the noon-day fire,—
Wildwood privacies, closets of lone desire,
Chamber from chamber parted with wavering arras of
    leaves,—
Cells for the passionate pleasure of prayer to the soul
    that grieves,
Pure with a sense of the passing of saints through the
    wood,
Cool for the dutiful weighing of ill with good;—

O braided dusks of the oak and woven shades of the
    vine,

While the riotous noon-day sun of the June-day long
   did shine
Ye held me fast in your heart and I held you fast in
   mine . . .

Ay, now, when my soul all day hath drunken the soul
   of the oak,
And my heart is at ease from men, and the wearisome
   sound of the stroke
  Of the scythe of time and the trowel of trade is low,
  And belief overmasters doubt, and I know that I
   know,
  And my spirit is grown to a lordly great compass
   within . . .
Oh now, unafraid, I am fain to face
  The vast sweet visage of space.
  To the edge of the wood I am drawn, I am drawn. . . .

The situation here is similar to that described in another poem by Lanier, "A Ballad of Trees and the Master,"
the first stanza of which reads as follows:

      Into the woods my Master went,
      Clean forspent, forspent.
      Into the woods my Master came,
      Forspent with love and shame.
      But the olives they were not blind to Him,
      The little gray leaves were kind to Him,
      The thorn-tree had a mind to Him,
      When into the woods He came.

In both poems, the forest affords a suitable, even helpful
place to pray, a place removed from the noisy world, a
place of privacy. The spaces between the trees are like
"cells." There is a suggestion of pathetic fallacy in the
statement that the leaves were "kind" to the Master. There
is indeed a hint of animism in Lanier's treatment of nature: it is as if a tree had a soul of its own ("my soul all day
hath drunken the soul of the oak"). But this is not the

pantheistic heresy which characterized so much nature
poetry of the nineteenth century, nor is it nature worship.
The relation between God and Nature in Lanier is not
one of identity. Lanier is not praying to a tree. God, to
whom his prayers are addressed, is clearly transcendent.
The relation of Lanier to the oak poses no more of a problem, perhaps, than the relation of St. Francis of Assisi to
the flowers and birds. It is, in either case, a sympathy felt by
one of God's creatures with another.

The important point for Lanier, at any rate, is that in an
age of pantheistic nature poetry, Lanier's God is not sub-
merged in the natural world. While it must be admitted
that Lanier attaches an exaggerated importance to nature
per se, it is an exaggeration which a poet of the nineteenth
century could hardly escape. It is highly significant, in the
present discussion, that he should have sought, in "A Ballad of Trees and the Master," a precedent, and authority,
for this importance in the life of Christ.

In the second part of "The Marshes of Glynn," the narrator comes out of the woods, and faces the marshes—"a
world of marsh that borders a world of sea." He faces what
lies before him "unafraid." The day's preparation in the
woods is rewarded. His religious faith is fortified by the
symbolism of the marsh hen, man's life and the marsh hen's
being alike in their precariousness:

As the marsh-hen secretly builds on the watery sod,
Behold I will build me a nest on the greatness of God:
I will fly in the greatness of God as the marsh hen flies
In the freedom that fills all the space 'twixt the marsh and
    the skies. . . .

The marsh hen is analogy only, and God's separateness from
nature is preserved. In the third part, the tide comes in at
sunset and covers the marshes, and the poem thus falls satis-
fyingly into the three phases: (1) spiritual preparation for
(2) this world (symbolized by the marshes) and for (3) the

world to come (symbolized by the sea). The second phase manages to suggest under the marsh imagery some convincing facets of the actual world, and the third is content to point merely to the mystery of the afterlife ("Who will reveal?" and "I would I could know").

Lanier reacted against the strictness of his Calvinistic heritage. Accordingly, his beloved marshes stand, to him, for the "liberal," the "catholic" attitude of mind. But there was nothing facile about this attitude in Lanier's case. There was struggle, pain, and heroism in Lanier's personal experience, and this comes out in the poem: the "catholic man" has "mightily won . . . good out of infinite pain."

Lanier aspired to "breadth." This aspiration, some have thought, was his downfall. The poet, they say, should strive for depth, not breadth; Whitman was broad; Dickinson, a much better poet, was deep. Those who say these things have a point. Lanier lacked not only Dickinson's depth but also her concentration and control. His work is marked by unrestraint, fancifulness, enthusiasm—traits which one associates with romanticism. But Lanier, I believe, had a saving Christian core.

"Somewhere between Emerson and Hawthorne," the reader may recall, is Allen Tate's attempt to locate Emily Dickinson theologically, and I should like to add that I prefer to think of her as nearer Hawthorne than Emerson; nearer, that is, the Puritan orthodoxy of Hawthorne than the romantic heterodoxy of Emerson.

Dickinson, to be sure, owes something to Emerson. Consider the following poem:

> Some keep the Sabbath going to church,
>   I keep it staying at home,
> With a bobolink for a chorister
>   And an orchard for a dome.
>
> Some keep the Sabbath in surplice,
>   I just wear my wings,

> And instead of tolling the bell for church
>   Our little sexton sings.
>
> God preaches—a noted clergyman,
>   And the sermon is never long;
> So instead of getting to heaven at last,
>   I'm going all along.

This has the anti-ecclesiastical tone of Emerson, recalling the remark in the *Divinity School Address* that "on Sundays, it seems wicked to go to church." The poem is also a part of the nature-cult (found, too, in Emerson) which regarded nature as uniformly beautiful and benign.[5]

Or consider this:

> I taste a liquor never brewed
> From tankards scooped in pearl;
> Not all the vats upon the Rhine
> Yield such an alcohol.

Here Dickinson has written her own paraphrase of Emerson's "Bacchus," a poem of transcendental intoxication, which begins: "Bring me wine, but wine which never grew/ In the belly of the grape. . . ."

But other poems—the better, deeper ones, I think—have Hawthorne's tone. For example:

> I like a look of agony,
> Because I know it's true;
> Men do not sham convulsion,
> Nor simulate a throe.
>
> The eyes glaze once, and that is death.
> Impossible to feign
> The beads upon the forehead
> By homely anguish strung.

It is too bad there is no concordance for Emily Dickinson's poetry, for if there were, we could look up "agony"

---

[5] Emily's "narrow fellow in the grass," though, suggests Hawthorne rather than Emerson.

and "anguish," and their equivalents (such as "pain," "suffering," "woe," "Gethsemane," "Calvary," and the like), and seeing how often such expressions occur in her 1,775 poems, we could infer how large a place pain and suffering occupied in her experience and view of life. We know without the statistics that the place was very large.

Suffering is pretty much absent in Emerson. There is suffering in Whitman, but more often than not one's attention is drawn not so much to the sufferer and his suffering as to the sympathetic vibration of the narrator. Suffering is central in Hawthorne: it is more than a means of setting in vibration a sympathetic response; it is educative, chastening, retributive, expiatory. "Surely," exclaimed Hester to Arthur near the end of *The Scarlet Letter*, "surely, we have ransomed one another, with all this woe!"

It would be interesting to investigate Dickinson's imagery to see how much of it derives from Christ in Gethsemane. The poem quoted above, "I like a look of agony," is a direct reference to Christ's suffering as described in St. Luke's Gospel: "And being in an agony he prayed more earnestly: and his sweat was as it were great drops of blood falling down to the ground." "Agony" is a key word in Dickinson, as is the associated word "Gethsemane." The latter occurs, for example, in a poem about "Currer Bell" (the pen name of Charlotte Brontë), whose work Dickinson admired. The lines go:

> Gathered from any wanderings,
>   Gethsemane can tell
> Through what transporting anguish
>   She reached the asphodel.

The Crucifixion, from the human standpoint, is high tragedy. The suffering of Christ is central to the Christian faith, and the cross is the Christian faith's central symbol. The note of suffering, then, and its spiritual fruits becomes a distinguishing mark in the present attempt to differentiate between the Christian and the non-Christian elements in our literature.

The latter part of this chapter has been concerned with showing, or attempting to show, that two poets, Lanier and Dickinson, while romantic in certain ways, may be regarded as Christian, too, or at least as containing important Christian elements. The emphasis in both poets on suffering and its efficacy, and especially on the archetypal suffering of Christ, seems almost decisive. Lanier's "Ballad" (Lanier can thus be drawn into a closer connection with his great New England contemporary) gave to romantic nature a new, poignant Christian application. If it seems ironic that Christ should have been slain on one of the "kind" trees, no betrayal was involved. Rather, the sacrifice of the tree's life along with the Master's made possible the greatest kindness of all.

IV   ✳   *Guilt and Innocence*

IF THE TWO chief romantics of nineteenth-century American literature were Emerson and Whitman, Hawthorne and Melville were the two chief counter-romantics. Henry James will be considered a counter-romantic also, for he inherited much from Hawthorne.

Neither Hawthorne nor Melville was in agreement with Emerson's philosophy. Hawthorne said, in "The Old Manse," that while he "admired Emerson as a poet of deep beauty and austere tenderness," he "sought nothing from him as a philosopher." Melville was intrigued by Emerson, but, like Hawthorne, rejected his philosophy. See, for example, the following remarks in a letter by Melville to his friend Evert Duyckinck, written in 1849, after hearing Emerson lecture:

I do not oscillate in Emerson's rainbow, but prefer rather to hang myself in mine own halter than swing in any other man's swing. Yet I think Emerson is more than a brilliant fellow. Be his stuff begged, borrowed, or stolen, or of his own domestic manufacture, he is an uncommon man. Swear he is a humbug —then he is no common humbug. . . . I love all men who *dive*. Any fish can swim near the surface, but it takes a great whale to go down stairs five miles or more. . . . I could readily see in Emerson, notwithstanding his merit, a gaping flaw. It was the insinuation that, had he lived in those days when the world was made, he might have offered some valu-

73

able suggestions. These men are all cracked right across the brow. . . . But enough of this Plato who talks thro' his nose.

Emerson seems not to have been aware of Melville; I know of no comment by him on Melville or his works. Of Hawthorne, Emerson had a good deal to say of a friendly nature in his *Journals,* but his remarks usually pertained to Hawthorne personally rather than to his writings. Of the latter, he said in 1842—and never recorded an altered opinion—that they "are good for nothing."

Neither Hawthorne nor Melville, apparently, ever commented on Whitman, and Whitman had not much to say about them. Of Melville, he said quite simply, in 1889, "I know little about him." Of Hawthorne, he said, "There is a morbid streak in him to which I can never accommodate myself." He went on to call him "a man of talent, even genius, even a master within certain limits." "Still," he reflected, "I think he is monotonous, he wears me out, I do not read him with pleasure." And in another passage (in *With Walt Whitman in Camden*), he called Hawthorne "morbid" again. Whitman's use of the word "morbid" is particularly interesting. It is an adjective which is often used by "optimistic" Americans; in fact, it has expressed the "optimistic" reaction to a great deal of truth-telling in literature.

If these two pairs—Emerson and Whitman, Hawthorne and Melville—occupied opposing camps and stood mutually apart, the members of the respective pairs regarded each other with favor and admiration. Each seems to have been conscious of a kind of alliance, one with the other. It was as if the lines of battle were firmly drawn, and each older writer had taken his stand, with a welcome and enthusiastic younger ally at his side. (Emerson was born in 1803; Hawthorne in 1804; Whitman in 1819; Melville in 1819.)

The Emerson-Whitman relationship has already been

touched upon. Emerson's famous letter (quoted above) is sufficient evidence on his side. Though his ardor cooled later, the change in attitude was for reasons apart from the main issues. Whitman addressed Emerson as "Dear Master" in the second edition of the *Leaves,* and the salutation and the letter that followed are an indication of true discipleship. Although some of Whitman's friends felt that Emerson failed Whitman later, Whitman never wavered in his belief in Emerson's true greatness.

A dramatic counterpart of discipleship in the opposing "alliance" is supplied by Melville's dedication of *Moby Dick* to Hawthorne, and Hawthorne's response, which is not extant, but which Melville referred to as "your joy-giving, exultation-breeding letter."

There is a great deal of friendship and admiration for Hawthorne in Melville's writings. There is, to begin with, Melville's great essay on Hawthorne, published pseudonymously in 1850, in which the lines of agreement are emphatically laid down. Here, after speaking of the "blackness" in Hawthorne, he continues:

Whether Hawthorne has simply availed himself of this mystical blackness as a means to the wondrous effects he makes it produce in his lights and shades; or whether there really lurks in him perhaps unknown to himself, a touch of Puritanic gloom, —this, I cannot altogether tell. Certain it is, however, that this great power of blackness in him derives its force from its appeal to that Calvinistic sense of Innate Depravity and Original Sin, from whose visitations, in some shape or other, no deeply thinking mind is always and wholly free. For, in certain moods, no man can weigh this world without throwing in something, somehow like Original Sin, to strike the uneven balance. At all events, perhaps no writer has ever wielded this terrific thought with greater terror than . . . Hawthorne. Still more: this black conceit pervades him through and through. You may be witched by his sunlight,—transported by the bright gildings in the skies he builds over you; but there is the black-

75

ness of darkness beyond; and even his bright gildings but fringe and play upon the edges of thunderclouds. . . . Now, it is that blackness in Hawthorne . . . that so fixes and fascinates me.

Melville goes on to find the same "blackness" in Shakespeare: ". . . this blackness it is that furnishes the infinite obscure of . . . that background against which Shakespeare plays his grandest conceits, the things which have made for Shakespeare his loftiest . . . renown, as the profoundest of thinkers. . . . It is those deep far-away things in him; those occasional flashings-forth of the intuitive Truth in him; those short, quick probings at the very axis of reality;—these are the things that make Shakespeare, Shakespeare." Melville hastened to add that he did not mean to imply that Hawthorne was as great as Shakespeare. But (writing in that nineteenth-century American atmosphere of all-is-good, all-is-well, which Emerson had helped so much to create, and finding a contrary view around him so rare, Edwards being a hundred years dead, and having left no worthy successor, and under such circumstances perhaps being all the more inclined to exaggerate the merits—great though they were—of Nathaniel Hawthorne) Melville ventured to declare that "the difference between the two men is by no means immeasureable." Mrs. Hawthorne was pleased with the comparison. Hawthorne himself, always clear-headed, said "The writer is no common man, and next to deserving his praise, it is good to have beguiled or bewitched such a man into praising me more than I deserve."

From May, 1850, until November, 1851, Hawthorne and Melville were near neighbors, Hawthorne living in Lenox, Massachusetts, in the red farmhouse overlooking the Stockbridge Bowl, and Melville living in Pittsfield, some six miles distant. A remarkable friendship soon developed, perhaps the most significant and fruitful in our literary history. Hawthorne had published *The Scarlet Letter* in the spring of 1850, and was therefore famous; he was soon busy with *The House of the Seven Gables,* which appeared early in 1851. Melville was deep in the throes of *Moby Dick,* which appeared (with the dedication to Hawthorne, as already noted) late in 1851. The two men visited back and forth a good deal, they talked far into the night (as Hawthorne said) "of time and eternity, books and publishers, and all possible and impossible matters," they drank gin, and smoked cigars.

The spirit of these sessions is suggested in an eloquent passage in one of Melville's letters, where he imagines a meeting in the next world under conditions more ideal, but (one must believe) not, so far as personal relations go, essentially different. The passage reads:

If ever, my dear Hawthorne, in the eternal times that are to come, you and I shall sit down in Paradise, in some little shady corner by ourselves; and if we shall by any means be able to smuggle a basket of champagne there (I won't believe in a Temperance Heaven), and if we shall then cross our celestial legs in the celestial grass that is forever tropical, and strike our glasses and our heads together, till both musically ring in concert,—then, O my dear fellow mortal, how shall we pleasantly discourse of all the things manifold which now so distress us, —when all the earth shall be but a reminiscence, yea, its final dissolution an antiquity.

The meetings of these two were lively and mutually stimulating. Though precise influences cannot be determined or proved, reciprocal influences there were, beyond a doubt. It is pleasant to think of the two books written during this period of friendly exchanges: *Moby Dick,* Melville's greatest, and *The House of the Seven Gables,* not Hawthorne's greatest (*The Scarlet Letter* is *that*), but at least—or so its author thought—his most "characteristic" production. Each man was to the other the best and most rewarding writer-friend whom he had known, or was ever to know.

Melville's letters to Hawthorne are among the most remarkable letters ever written. It is regrettable that none of Hawthorne's to Melville have survived. But we do have references to Melville in Hawthorne's *Notebooks;* in the notebook kept in the Berkshires there are accounts of meetings, journeys taken together, conversations; and in the English journal, there is this sad, moving account of the meeting in 1856 at Liverpool (where Hawthorne was Consul), which proved to be their last:

Melville stayed with us from Tuesday till Thursday; and, on the intervening day, we took a pretty long walk together, and sat down in a hollow among the sand hills (sheltering ourselves from the high, cool wind) and smoked a cigar. Melville, as he always does, began to reason of Providence and futurity, and of everything that lies beyond human ken, and informed me that he had "pretty much made up his mind to be annihilated"; but still he does not seem to rest in that anticipation; and, I think, will never rest until he gets hold of a definite belief. It is strange how he persists—and has persisted ever since I knew him, and probably long before—in wandering to-and-fro over these deserts, as dismal and monotonous as the sand hills amid which we were sitting. He can neither believe, nor be comfortable in his unbelief; and he is too honest and courageous not to try to do one or the other.

This fine passage is, in truth, almost equally applicable to Hawthorne himself. For Hawthorne, like Melville, had reasoned much concerning Providence and futurity and the things which lie beyond human ken. It was Hawthorne's dilemma, as well as Melville's, to find it difficult either to believe or to be comfortable in unbelief. "Lord, I believe; help thou mine unbelief" has been the prayer of many a good doubting Christian since it was first prayed in *St. Mark*'s Gospel by the father of the possessed child. There can indeed be no Christian faith worthy of the name (unless it be among the cherubim and seraphim) without this struggle between belief and unbelief, and there can be no true human sympathy without it.

The concept of Original Sin runs through all of Hawthorne. His story "The Birthmark" is one of the better illustrations of the idea.

Georgiana's otherwise perfect beauty is marred by a tiny blemish (shaped like a hand) on her cheek. Aylmer, her husband, who is a "scientist," is more and more disturbed by this blemish, for Aylmer is a perfectionist, a doctrinaire. He is also a man who is ambitious for success and fame in his profession. If he could remove this one imperfection (and he thinks he can), several advantages would accrue to him: (1) he would have created, in a sense, something new under the sun, namely, a perfect being; (2) he would have satisfied his desire for perfection; and (3) he would have satisfied his desire for power.

His wife submits to the trial. He brings to bear on the problem all of his experimental resources. He tries, and fails. For just as the hand fades away and at last completely disappears, Georgiana dies. The grief of Aylmer is equivocal: it is partly for the loss of his wife, and quite as much (one suspects a good deal more) for the failure of his experiment.

It is interesting that Aylmer was in the beginning the only one concerned about the mark. Georgiana herself was not unhappy about it—that is, until Aylmer became unhappy, and then her unhappiness was owing to his unhappiness rather than the mark itself. Before her marriage, Georgiana's other suitors had positively admired the mark. They thought it actually enhanced her beauty. They would have been most grateful for the privilege of kissing it. What wise, sensible lads *they* were!

If one asks, Is not Aylmer's pursuit of perfection worthy of all praise? The answer must be, yes, and no. The admiration of perfection is praiseworthy, but Aylmer was trying

to make over another human being. This was a presumptuous sin. It was a usurpation of the role of Creator.
Aylmer, moreover, sees imperfection in Georgiana, but
not in himself. He richly deserves Jesus' rebuke, "Thou
hypocrite, cast out first the beam out of thine own eye,
and then shalt thou see clearly to pull out the mote that
is in thy brother's eye." Georgiana, in charity and love,
does not blame Aylmer; she praises him, rather, with her
last breath. "You have aimed loftily," she said. But the
author judges differently. "Had Aylmer reached a profounder wisdom," he says, "he need not thus have flung
away the happiness which would have woven his mortal
life of the selfsame texture with the celestial."

What is this "profounder wisdom"? Well, for one thing,
the acceptance, even the cherishing, of human imperfection. Georgiana's birthmark is a symbol of human imperfection, it is the mark of her humanity, it shows her to be
human. It is a symbol, in theological language, of Original
Sin. Not that Georgiana is guilty of any overt sinful acts;
she is the soul of goodness and devotion. The term Original Sin doesn't refer primarily to overt sinful acts, as such
acts are ordinarily understood. It means basic human nature, fallible, imperfect human nature; it means the state
of being human; it means that we live in an imperfect,
non-ideal world.

If the question is asked, Well, if the mark is the sign of
imperfection, wherein was Georgiana imperfect? the answer is not too difficult. Her "error" was perhaps putting
her trust in a man unworthy of that trust, or putting in
mortal man a trust which belongs to God alone. Possibly
she succumbed too, the least bit, to vanity (she would
hardly be "human" if she didn't), to the attraction in the
idea of being the only "perfect" one. But the trust and
the vanity endear her all the more to those who have a
true appreciation of the fact that man was created a little

lower than the angels. What a stupid, wicked fellow Aylmer was, after all, with his talk about perfection! In seeking to mend all with one conceited stroke, he marred all, utterly and irredeemably.

Like Aylmer, Dr. Rappaccini (in the tale, "Rappaccini's Daughter") was a perfectionist of a sort. He, too, undertook to remake a fellow creature, Beatrice, his daughter, usurping the role of the Creator. The good Doctor had an advanced educational scheme. By segregating Beatrice from the rest of her kind, and giving her a special course of instruction, he hoped to produce a superwoman. Accordingly, he isolated her in a garden filled with beautiful poisonous plants. (How modern all this sounds!) As the girl gradually assimilated the poison, she was able to handle the plants without harm to herself. Her body finally became so thoroughly impregnated with poison that her breath was fatal to insects, and her touch left a purple mark on the wrist of a "normal" young man who fell in love with her. Beatrice died when she was given an "antidote." The Doctor's grandiose and presumptuous scheme had failed, just as Aylmer's had failed. Rappaccini and Aylmer alike were great sinners. Their sin was the sin of intellectual arrogance. Beatrice was a victim. But she was also, to a certain extent, an accomplice, and the poison in her body may symbolize the pride generated by her isolated way of life.

The positive force of the evil principle is always at work in Hawthorne's fictions. The snake or serpent (symbolizing the Devil) is one of his central symbols. In Dr. Rappaccini's garden the luxurious plants extended themselves serpentlike along the ground. The stranger in the tale "Young Goodman Brown" carries a walking stick which resembles a serpent. This stranger turns out to be the Devil himself. Emphasis upon the Devil as an active agent in the world is, I think, a necessary point of Christian doctrine. Hawthorne takes over the New Testament concept of diabolical possession; many of his characters are "possessed of the Devil." The young man in the tale "Egotism, or the Bosom Serpent" was possessed until the devil was finally driven out, or exorcised. Goodman Brown was possessed, in a somewhat different way.

Brown met up with the Devil, disguised as a kindly old man, at the edge of the forest at nightfall, and was persuaded to accompany the old man deep into the forest to attend a witch meeting. He was not too hard to persuade; he had in fact planned to do this very thing. When he got to the witch meeting, which was a gaudy affair, he saw, or thought he saw, all the pious folk of the village, including his own wife, Faith. It is never quite clear whether Brown takes the final vows of allegiance at the Devil's altar, nor does it much matter. He has had his vision of evil, and the experience has a permanent traumatic effect. Not all of Hawthorne's young men, however, are crushed by the knowledge of evil. Young Robin, for example, in "My Kinsman, Major Molineux," survives a somewhat similar experience, and appears to be the stronger for it.

What is the purpose of evil in the world? It is a question which Hawthorne asks over and over again, and with special emphasis in his last completed fiction. "Is sin then like sorrow," Kenyon asks in *The Marble Faun*, "an element of human education, through which we struggle to a higher and purer state than we could otherwise have attained? Did Adam fall, that we might ultimately rise to a far loftier paradise than his?" It is Milton's concern in the last book of *Paradise Lost*, where Adam says:

> Full of doubt I stand
> Whether I should repent me now of sin
> By me done and occasioned, or rejoice
> Much more that much more good thereof shall spring
> To God more glory, more good-will to men
> From God—and over wrath grace shall abound.

St. Paul had raised the same question. "Shall we continue in sin," he asks, "that grace may abound?" And answers, "God forbid." But he had previously said that "where sin abounded, grace did much more abound." Allied to this view is the doctrine of the *felix culpa,* the happy fault, or fortunate fall, which regards the fall of man as fortunate because, if he had not fallen, he would never have known the inestimable benefits of redemption. The doctrine is an old Catholic one, of course, and we have seen its elaboration by Milton and Hawthorne. If sin may seem to abound more than grace in Hawthorne, and the fall appear more often unhappy than happy, it must be borne in mind that in an inquiry of this sort, we are not concerned with superficial or worldly criteria. If there is spiritual growth, however painfully achieved (and it cannot be achieved without pain), grace can be said much more to abound, and the fall can be said to have been fortunate. Grace much more abounds, for example, and the fall proves fortunate, in *The Scarlet Letter,* though a worldly appraisal would point to a different view.

One of the chief thematic tensions in Hawthorne is the tension between the Puritan and the romantic tendencies. Hawthorne's writings lean in the Puritan direction. But he lived in a romantic age, and his work shows an awareness of the temper of that age. His work is in a sense a "criticism" of that temper, but it is not a criticism which is blind to the romantic fascination, or refuses it a sympathetic hearing.

In *The Scarlet Letter,* Hester is spokesman for the romantic view, and her argument carries weight with many readers. Here is a woman—handsome, of a voluptuous beauty—who as a young girl was talked into marrying an old man, Roger Chillingworth, a medical doctor and a cold, intellectual scientist, who must have proved unsatisfactory as a husband. She came alone to Boston, Massachusetts (in the 1630's), and fell in love with the brilliant,

83

popular young clergyman, Arthur Dimmesdale. They had a love affair, the offspring of which was a girl baby whom her mother named Pearl (from the Biblical "pearl of great price"). The stiffnecked Puritan community condemned Hester, and required her to wear on the bosom of her dress at all times the red letter A, standing for Adulteress. Chillingworth arrived just after the birth of the child, to haunt Hester and persecute the minister, for he sensed infallibly that Dimmesdale was the child's father. Hester was a woman of great strength—"a damn fine woman," one appreciative commentator has called her. She bore up well under her trials. She became a sister of mercy, and, eventually, a respected figure in this bigoted town.

Meanwhile, the sensitive, conscientious minister was paying a high price for his secret. Chillingworth, whose identity as Hester's husband was not known to Dimmesdale for a long while, preyed upon the minister's mind and soul in sinister, insidious ways. And then, after seven long years (Hester serving, Arthur suffering), the lovers meet in the forest—one can imagine at the place of their first rendezvous. Hester tells Arthur who Chillingworth is, and begs and wins Arthur's forgiveness for not having told him at the beginning (she had promised Chillingworth that she wouldn't tell, and had conspired with him all this time to keep the poor minister in the dark). And then she urges a course of immediate action: that the three of them embark on the ship at that moment in Boston harbor, and flee to Europe. The minister agrees, caught up in the old passion. But the story doesn't turn out that way. Arthur on the morrow, after preaching the "Election Sermon" before the Governor, Magistrates, and general populace, mounts the scaffold where Hester was made to stand in ignominy seven years before, confesses his adultery to the breathless, incredulous multitude, and dies.

This much of a synopsis has seemed necessary to remind

the reader of the setting of the famous speech by Hester which I propose to call "romantic." The occasion was the forest meeting, just referred to, and the words spoken by Hester were these: "What we did had a consecration of its own. We felt it so! We said so to each other."

Hester never felt that she had sinned, and her speech is very appealing. Is not the book after all, some readers ask, an exposé of Puritan bigotry and intolerance? The answer is, Yes, to be sure; *The Scarlet Letter* is a criticism of Puritanism as well as of romanticism. But when the romantic apologist goes on to insist that the book is a vindication of individual impulse, the right of the individual to happiness, the sacredness of passion, it is necessary to demur. Does not Hester's view carry individualism a bit too far? Does it not translate "the sacredness of the individual" into "the individual a law unto himself"? The book, taken as a whole, does not support the romantic view. I say this almost regretfully, because I like Hester and I sympathize (who does not?) with her frustrated love. But it is a "romantic" sympathy. *A consecration of its own?* "Alas that ever love was sin!" Hester is far removed from Chaucer's Wife of Bath (Hester is no wanton), but when thinking of her plight, one remembers the Wife's famous lament.

The tension between Puritan and romantic is especially emphasized in the forest scene. The symbolism is dualistic. The forest itself has a double significance: it stands for moral error, being the place where Hester and Arthur go astray; and it stands for natural innocence, for here little Pearl becomes a child of nature (in the romantic sense) and is recognized as such by the creatures of the forest. Pearl herself is also double: not only is she an innocent child of nature, but she is at the same time an agent of retribution (she insists that Hester replace the scarlet letter on her dress after having cast it aside). Hester's casting of the let-

85

ter aside was her "romantic revolt"; [1] her replacing of the letter was her outward compliance with (not inward acceptance of) the Puritan law. Throughout the forest scene (perhaps the most richly symbolic scene in the book), Hester stands for romantic individualism, and Arthur for the claims of law and conscience.

For although Arthur, stimulated by the excitement of the moment, agrees to Hester's plan of escape, his experiences after leaving Hester force him back into the Puritan path. On re-entering the village, he was sorely tempted by the devil to say blasphemous things to the passers-by. On reaching his room, he destroyed the manuscript of the Election Sermon to be delivered on the following day, and furiously set about writing a fresh sermon. The author does not tell us exactly what went on in Arthur's mind at this point. To do so would be almost unavoidably to prepare us too well for the climactic scene, the public confession, and sacrifice the element of legitimate surprise and shock. But though we are not told explicitly, we can be sure that there was a struggle, and the minister was able finally to beat down Satan under his feet. It is axiomatic with Hawthorne that there can be no virtue without conflict and struggle. Only a great struggle can account for the minister's great heroism, and the greatness of the struggle came out of the greatness of his despair, his extremity.

I have said that Arthur stood for the claims of the Puritan law. "Christian" can be used here interchangeably (as so often in a discussion of this kind) with "Puritan." The reader hardly needs to be told that the "law" broken by Hester and Arthur was the Seventh Commandment of the Decalogue, and that the Decalogue was not abrogated by the New Testament dispensation. Adultery continued to be a sin after Christ, as it had been before Christ. Jesus *forgave* the woman taken in adultery. The Puritans did

[1] Hester might have said with Emerson (in "Self-Reliance"), "I do not wish to expiate, but to live."

not invent the Seventh Commandment, nor were they un-Christian in insisting upon its importance, though an un-informed reader might infer both of these notions from some of the commentaries on *The Scarlet Letter*. The Puritan community in Hawthorne's novel was un-Christian in its unforgiving attitude and behavior—its bigotry and cruelty—but it was not un-Christian in its doctrine.

Hester is a romantic heroine, a splendid one. She has been much admired, and justifiably. The richly embroidered A has been called by one of her modern admirers "the red badge of courage." She was indeed courageous, and strong. Arthur, in comparison, has seemed pitiably weak, but justice, I think, has not been done to Arthur. Arthur's situation was much more difficult than Hester's. Her conflict was external. She was integrated within herself, and she set her solidly united self resolutely against the intolerant community. A fight like this can be inspiriting; it is fortifying, it builds one up. But Arthur's fight was with himself. His was a state of civil war, not war with the outside world. The community idolized him, but he had his internal troubles, and these proved to be serious. (Psychiatrists who happen to read *The Scarlet Letter* often express surprise that Hawthorne, in 1850, should have understood how serious internal conflicts can be.) If heroism is measured in terms of the magnitude and severity of the struggle which is undergone, then Arthur must be adjudged the more heroic of the two, for Hester never did anything which cost a tithe of the bloody sweat, the agony, which Arthur's public confession cost.

Hester is a noble, frustrated, pathetic figure, but she is not a tragic figure, because her mind is made up. My hat is off to her as high as the highest; Wordsworth's words fit her beautifully—"A perfect Woman, nobly planned/ To warn, to comfort, and command." But she is not the protagonist, the chief actor, and the tragedy of *The Scarlet Letter* is not her tragedy but Arthur's.

He is the persecuted one, the tempted one. He it was whom the sorrows of death encompassed, the pains of hell gat hold upon. His public confession is one of the noblest climaxes of tragic literature. Poor, bedevilled Arthur Dimmesdale, the slave of passion and the servant of the Lord, brilliant of intellect, eloquent of voice, the darling of his congregation, the worst of hypocrites, and the prey of endless rationalizations and sophistries! No veteran of the cavalry of woe was ever more battle-scarred or desperate than Dimmesdale as he stood on the scaffold, and began, "People of New England!" "with a voice that rose over them, high, solemn, majestic."

The confession was decisive. Its function in the novel is to resolve the action. It turned the scales in the great debate, though Hester, romantic heretic to the last, remained unconvinced, impenitent, unredeemed. She had at best an imperfect understanding of Arthur's problem. As for Arthur, he saw the problem all too clearly. He must make a public confession: "Confess your faults one to another . . . that ye may be healed." There could be no salvation without that. Arthur was saved, yet as by fire. He was truly a firebrand plucked out of the burning. The confession brought about a reconciliation with God and man; with, not least, little Pearl, from whom there had been a complete estrangement. "Pearl kissed his lips. A spell was broken." Hester watched, wonderingly. "Thou lookest far into eternity, with those bright dying eyes," she said; "Tell me what thou seest." What Arthur saw chiefly was God's mercy: "He is merciful," he said; "He hath proved His mercy most of all in my afflictions. . . . Praised be His name! His will be done!"

Thus in his profoundest character-creation, and in the resolution of his greatest book, Hawthorne has employed the Christian thesis: "Father, not my will, but thine be done." And in the scene so constructed, we see the best illustration of what Melville called, perceptively, "the ever-moving dawn that forever advances through Hawthorne's darkness, and circumnavigates his world."

It is time now to look at Melville.

Melville said to Hawthorne, after the completion of *Moby Dick,* "I have written a wicked book, and feel as spotless as the lamb." If Melville felt justified in what he had written, why did he call *Moby Dick* "a wicked book"?

Perhaps because he had written a book with a wicked protagonist. The protagonist, to be sure, is punished for his wickedness. Still, what if he is presented sympathetically, admiringly, as a hero, or something of a hero? Then perhaps the book becomes "a wicked book" in the eyes of its author. Melville's case recalls Milton's, in *Paradise Lost,* where Satan appears in a heroic light in the early part of the poem. Melville's description of Ahab, in fact, often seems reminiscent of Milton's description of Satan. Both are superheroes, archangelic though fallen, battle-scarred, vindictive, bent on revenge. Might not Milton have thought that *Paradise Lost* through Book Two was a wicked book? Is not the treatment of Satan in those tremendous opening scenes too sympathetic to comport strictly with Christian piety? Possibly Melville felt this about his treatment of Ahab, the great difference being that while Milton does get around, in due course, to debasing Satan, Ahab, though defeated and destroyed at last, is never debased: his stature is of heroic proportions to the end.

What manner of man is Ahab?

One of the best answers to this question is given in the remarks of Captain Peleg to Ishmael in Chapter XVI, before the start of the voyage, and before the *Pequod's* captain has appeared on the scene. "He's a queer man, Captain Ahab," says Peleg,

"so some think—but a good one. Oh, thou'lt like him well enough; no fear, no fear. He's a grand, ungodly, god-like man,

Captain Ahab; doesn't speak much; but, when he does speak, then you may well listen. Mark ye, be forewarned; Ahab's above the common; Ahab's been in colleges, as well as 'mong the cannibals; been used to deeper wonders than the waves; fixed his fiery lance in mightier, stranger foes than whales. His lance! aye, the keenest and the surest that, out of all our isle! Oh! he ain't Captain Bildad; no, and he ain't Captain Peleg; *he's Ahab,* boy; and Ahab of old, thou knowest, was a crowned king!"

To which young Ishmael replied: "And a very vile one. When that wicked king was slain, the dogs, did they not lick his blood?" And Peleg continued:

"Come hither to me—hither, hither. Look ye lad; never say that on board the Pequod. Never say it anywhere. Captain Ahab did not name himself. . . . I know Captain Ahab well; I've sailed with him as mate years ago; I know what he is— a good man—not a pious, good man like Bildad, but a swearing good man—something like me—only there's a good deal more of him. Aye, aye, I know that he was never very jolly; and I know that on the passage home, he was a little out of his mind for a spell; but it was the sharp shooting pains in his bleeding stump that brought that about, as anyone might see. I know, too, that ever since he lost his leg last voyage by that accursed whale, he's been a kind of moody—desperate moody, and savage sometimes; but that will all pass off. And once for all, let me tell thee and assure thee, young man, it's better to sail with a moody good captain than a laughing bad one. So good-bye to thee—and wrong not Captain Ahab, because he happens to have a wicked name. Besides, my boy, he has a wife—not three voyages wedded—a sweet resigned girl. Think of that; by that sweet girl, that old man has a child: hold ye then there can be any utter, hopeless harm in Ahab? No, no, my lad; stricken, blasted, if he be, Ahab has his humanities!"

This is one man's opinion, but an impressive one. We are not to suppose that the author necessarily endorses it, in its entirety. Neither should we identify Melville with any of his characters—with Captain Peleg, or Ishmael, or Ahab even. Like all great imaginative works, *Moby Dick* is essentially dramatic in character, and its meaning will be found, not in a single scene or character or speech, but in its totality. Nevertheless, as we pursue our course through the book, we will recall Peleg's account of this "ungodly, god-like man."

Ishmael's description of Ahab (in Chapter XXVIII), after his first sight of him, is even more powerful:

He looked like a man cut away from the stake, when the fire has overrunningly wasted all the limbs without consuming them, or taking away one particle from their compacted aged robustness. His whole high, broad form, seemed made of solid bronze, and shaped in an unalterable mould, like Cellini's cast Perseus. Threading its way out from among his grey hairs, and continuing right down one side of his tawny scorched face and neck, till it disappeared in his clothing, you saw a slender rod-like mark, lividly whitish. It resembled that perpendicular seam sometimes made in the straight, lofty trunk of a great tree, when the upper lightning tearingly darts down it, and without wrenching a single twig, peels and grooves out the bark from top to bottom, ere running off into the soil, leaving the tree still greenly alive, but branded.

One opinion had it that this scar was a "birth-mark," which extended "from crown to sole"; another, that it had been received "in an elemental strife at sea." The description of the mark, whatever its origin, recalls particularly Milton's Satan, who was driven over the battlements of Heaven scarred by God's thunderbolts.

Ahab's obsessive desire is vengeance on Moby Dick, and he incites his crew to unite with him in this mad enterprise. No Hitler ever poured forth such hysterical, compelling eloquence. "And this is what ye have shipped for, men!" he shouted; "to chase that white whale on both sides of land, and over all sides of earth, till he spouts black blood and rolls fin out" (Chapter XXXVI). When

Starbuck, the only man on the *Pequod* who is not swept off his feet by Ahab's fury, remonstrates that "vengeance on a dumb brute . . . seems blasphemous," Ahab replies, in one of the great key passages:

All visible objects, man, are but as pasteboard masks. But in each event—in the living act, the undoubted deed—there, some unknown but still reasoning thing puts forth the mouldings of its features from behind the unreasoning mask. If a man will strike, strike through the mask! How can the prisoner reach outside except by thrusting through the wall? To me, the white whale is that wall, shoved near to me. Sometimes I think there's naught beyond. But 'tis enough. He tasks me; he heaps me; I see in him outrageous strength, with an inscrutable malice sinewing it. That inscrutable thing is chiefly what I hate; and be the white whale agent, or be the white whale principal, I will wreak that hate upon him. Talk not to me of blasphemy, man; I'd strike the sun if it insulted me.

One doesn't go very far into the book without having to face up, at least tentatively, to the question, What does the White Whale stand for? It is a question which one should not be in too great a hurry to answer definitively (if indeed a definitive answer can be found), but it must be entertained, for the story soon takes on large symbolic dimensions. In the former encounter with the White Whale, we are told, Moby Dick, "suddenly sweeping his sickle-shaped lower jaw beneath him . . . had reaped away Ahab's leg, as a mower a blade of grass in the field. No turbaned Turk, no hired Venetian or Malay could have smote him with more seeming malice." "Seeming," of course, leaves some doubt as to whether the malice was real.

"Ever since that almost fatal encounter," the narrator continues (Chapter XLI),

Ahab had cherished a wild vindictiveness against the whale, all the more fell for that in his frantic morbidness he at last came to identify with him, not only all his bodily woes, but all his intellectual and spiritual exasperations. The White Whale swam before him as the monomaniac incarnation of all those malicious agencies which some deep men feel eating in them, till they are left living on with half a heart and half a lung. That intangible malignity which has been from the beginning; to whose dominion even the modern Christians ascribe one-half of the world; which the ancient Ophites of the east reverenced in their statue devil;—Ahab did not fall down and worship it like them; but deliriously transferring its idea to the abhorred white whale, he pitted himself, all mutilated, against it. All that most maddens and torments; all that stirs up the lees of things; all truth with malice in it; all that cracks the sinews and cakes the brain; all the subtle demonisms of life and thought; all evil, to crazy Ahab, was visibly personified, and made practically assailable in Moby Dick. He piled upon the whale's white hump the sum of all the general rage and hate felt by his whole race from Adam down; and then, as if his chest had been a mortar, he burst his hot heart's shell upon it.

The White Whale was all these things to Ahab. But Ahab, we notice, is the victim of a "wild vindictiveness," a "frantic morbidness." Ahab is, according to the narrator, a "monomaniac," and indeed "crazy"—"all evil, to *crazy* Ahab, was visibly personified, and made practically assailable in Moby Dick."

Ishmael is technically the narrator, but in many parts of the book he is hardly acceptable as such, for it isn't entirely clear how he could have had the requisite knowledge. In the passage just quoted, for example, he was not an eye witness to the encounter with Moby Dick, yet it is described with circumstantial detail. One is compelled to regard the "point of view" as vacillating between restricted and omniscient. The story, that is to say, is told on the authority, sometimes of Ishmael, and sometimes of the author himself. In trying to interpret the reality before us, we are not much concerned with making allow-

93

ance for Ishmael's aberrations of vision (he is too neutral a character), but we must make an allowance for Ahab's.

The question may well be asked, Is what the White Whale stands for to Ahab, what the White Whale stands for? And the answer must be, Yes, in part, certainly, despite Ahab's "monomania" and "craziness." Much madness is divinest sense. But the meaning of the Whale, though incorporating Ahab's meaning, is not necessarily confined to it.

In that remarkable chapter on "The Whiteness of the Whale" (Chapter XLII), we have (is it on Ishmael's authority, or the author's?) a discourse which sets forth with an amazing wealth of illustration the ambiguity of whiteness. One connotation of whiteness is benign: the bridal veil, the white hairs of old age, the ermine of the judge, the alb (from the Latin *alba*, white) of the Christian priest. But there are forms of whiteness which are sinister, and strike terror to the soul: the polar bear, the albatross (which Coleridge's poem made an omen of evil in the popular imagination), the Albino man, the corpse, the shroud, the ghost. Is reality, then, an ambiguity, a dualism? Is whiteness both benign and malignant? Must Ahab's report be corrected for astigmatism? Must Goodman Brown's, because after the traumatic experience of the witch-meeting he could see nothing but evil around him? Ahab's meeting with the whale was traumatic, too, and the two "meetings" are allegorically comparable, with the difference that Brown, finding no foe "visibly personified and practically assailable," succumbed to despair. The two fables indeed make an illuminating comparison, and it is interesting to recall that Melville was strongly attracted to "Young Goodman Brown," saying in the essay already quoted from that Hawthorne's tale is as "deep as Dante."

Ahab's moral character deteriorates in the course of the story. Progressively he stifles "his humanities." He rejects, one by one, the good influences: Starbuck, Pip, thoughts

94

of home, wife, child. He comes progressively under the domination of Fedallah, the Parsee, who is the Devil, or the Devil's efficient emissary.

Chapter CXIII, "The Forge," is a scene of powerful diabolism. As the Parsee looks on, the blacksmith forges a new harpoon for Ahab, who then anoints the barb with the blood of the "heathen" harpooners, Tashtego, Queequeg, and Daggoo, and "as the malignant iron scorchingly devours the baptismal blood," he "deliriously howls" the wicked words, "Ego non baptizo te in nomine patris, sed in nomine diaboli" ("I baptize you not in the name of the father but in the name of the devil"). One recalls the devil's baptismal service in "Young Goodman Brown."

Shortly afterwards, the *Pequod* is surrounded by a great electrical storm, and the yardarms are alive with St. Elmo's fire. While each yardarm blazes with a "tri-pointed trinity of flames" (as if to mock the Holy Trinity), Ahab puts his foot upon the Parsee (as if to defy even the Devil), and speaks these blasphemous words:

"Oh! thou clear spirit of clear fire, whom on these seas I as Persian once did worship, till in the sacramental act so burned by thee, that to this hour I bear the scar; I now know thee, thou clear spirit, and I now know that thy right worship is defiance. . . . In the midst of the personified impersonal, a personality stands here. . . . Oh, thou clear spirit, of thy fire thou madest me, and like a true child of fire, I breathe it back to thee. . . . Leap! leap up, and lick the sky! I leap with thee; I burn with thee; would fain be welded with thee; defyingly I worship thee!"

In the summer of 1851, while Melville was writing *Moby Dick,* he read Hawthorne's "Ethan Brand," the story of a man who had brought about such an imbalance in his own nature by cultivating the "head" (he became a great "philosopher") to the neglect of the "heart," that he at length committed suicide by jumping into a flaming lime-kiln. As Brand stood poised above the fiery furnace of the kiln, he spoke a speech somewhat like the one by Ahab, just quoted. "Come, deadly element of Fire, henceforth my familiar [2] friend!" he cried; "Embrace me, as I do thee!"

Melville may have been influenced by Hawthorne's story. The two characters are dissimilar in some respects, but basically similar. Brand does not have Ahab's defiance, and Ahab is not intellectually cold like Brand—he is the most impassioned of men. But both are fire-worshippers, Devil worshippers. As Brand spoke, "blue flames played upon his face, and imparted a wild and ghastly light," recalling the St. Elmo phosphorescence on board the *Pequod*. Both Ahab and Brand made, in effect, a Faustian pact; they exchanged their souls for the Devil's help. Both are monomaniacs—Ahab is a raving one; Brand is cold, impassive, uncommunicative. Both are suicides, for Ahab's last assault on the Whale is made with suicidal recklessness. Ahab is the more "sympathetic" of the two, the more heroic, the more admirable (we admire, sympathize with, Brand scarcely at all), and Ahab's imbalance is owing not to the lack of passion, as in Brand's case, but to the excess of it. But both are colossal egotists, full of pride, and both are guilty (though Ahab is not destitute of "feeling," as Brand) of what Hawthorne called "the unpardonable sin," in that both had severed all human ties.

We need not suppose that Melville "approved" of Ahab. He undoubtedly "admired" this hero, this Titan of men (the creative artist is entitled to the privilege of admiring his own creation), but he did not necessarily approve of him, anymore than Shakespeare necessarily approved of Macbeth, or Milton of Satan. Ahab is diabolical, anti-Christian, and, like Macbeth and Satan, he has a hellish fall.

From the moral standpoint, he is not an example but a warning. He illustrates both man's powers, and their misuse. He is romantic individualism carried to the last de-

---

[2] "Familiar" has the force here of "attendant devil."

gree. He is the selfish monopolist, the dictator with a genius for controlling people, an anti-social monster. F.O. Matthiessen saw in him, interestingly enough, an anticipation of that undesirable product of nineteenth-century individualism in America, the tycoon. Ahab is without laughter, and sick with the sickness of monomania. He is hopelessly, tragically self-involved.

One remembers, upon reaching the end of the book, Father Mapple's sermon (in Chapter IX), and looking back, one sees its importance more clearly than before. For Father Mapple's sermon about Jonah gives us a yardstick by which to measure the sin of Ahab. The preacher recapitulated the Biblical story as "a story of the sin, hardheartedness, suddenly awakened fears, the swift punishment, repentance, prayers, and finally the deliverance and joy of Jonah." The latter part of this sequence, of course, has no parallel in the story of Ahab: Ahab did not repent, he did not pray (to God), he was not delivered. Father Mapple put the difficulty as follows: "If we obey God, we must disobey ourselves; and it is in this disobeying ourselves, wherein the hardness of obeying God consists." Ahab could not obey God because he could not disobey himself.

And what of the Whale? The Whale may be, of course, a number of things. It may be, I suppose, some kind of obstacle to man's fulfilment. It is no mere physical obstacle, but possibly one of our own monomaniacal creation. Or perhaps the Whale stands for the inscrutable, the last mystery which man strives to wring from the heart of the universe, and in so doing, like Marlowe's Dr. Faustus, attempts "more than Heavenly power permits." Or possibly the Whale stands not so much for an unachievable or impossible aim as one which is not achieved in this instance because Ahab goes about it in the wrong way. Faulkner's *The Bear* tells of a successful "hunt" which is conducted in a very different spirit from Ahab's: with

97

decorum, reverence, humility. The Bear, like the Whale, is a great mythical creature; both are surrounded by an aura of the supernatural. The chief difference between the two stories is in the spirit of the pursuit: it is the difference between anarchistic individualism and tradition, vengeance and respect, blasphemy and piety, defiance and acceptance.

Moby Dick is the greatest classic, in America, of man's defiance. Man is prone to defiance; it is another manifestation, and a chief one, of Original Sin. Paradoxically, man's great heroisms and his great crimes spring from the same source. Melville's concept of human nature (like Shakespeare's) is a heroic one. Man is capable of great heights and great depths, and he could not be capable of the one without being capable of the other also.

The extremes of height and depth are illustrated in *Billy Budd,* a much shorter work than *Moby Dick,* but almost as famous, and almost as great. It was written nearly forty years after *Moby Dick,* during the last years of the author's life, and published posthumously.

Billy Budd was a handsome young sailor on board His Majesty's Ship the *Indomitable* during the Napoleonic Wars. He was accused falsely by the Master-at-Arms, Claggart, of plotting a mutiny, whereupon he instinctively struck Claggart a fatal blow. In the trial which followed, Captain Vere, though sympathetically disposed toward Billy, and morally certain that Claggart had lied, felt compelled to insist upon the death penalty, and Billy was hanged.

In the creation of Billy, Melville appears to have been influenced by Hawthorne's "The Birthmark," for in the story, he writes: "Though our Handsome Sailor had as much of masculine beauty as one can expect anywhere to see; nevertheless, like the beautiful woman in one of Hawthorne's minor tales, there was just one thing amiss in him. No visible blemish, indeed, as with the lady; no, but an occasional liability to a vocal defect." In short, in moments of emotional stress, Billy stuttered.

It might be interesting to explore a bit the parallel which Melville himself suggests. A physical defect, in each case, is a symbol of human imperfection, of one's being human. Without the flaw, the person would be inhumanly perfect. The flaw, therefore, becomes a symbol of Original Sin. Both Georgiana and Billy, to be sure, are "innocent," apparently without guile, but the very guilelessness may lead to complicity. If Georgiana had not had the tiny hand on her cheek, she would not have conspired in its removal; if Billy had not been a stutterer, he would not have struck Claggart, for the vocal block seemed to trigger the blow. The flaw in each case closely concerns one's *amour propre,* one's vanity. Neither Georgiana nor Billy, though guileless, is quite unself-conscious, and in self-conscious moments the physical defect becomes more prominent: the red hand shows forth more boldly against the surrounding paleness, the speech impediment becomes an out-and-out stutter, or worse. Might these marks symbolize a kind of vanity, the more insidious for its unobtrusiveness? Might these persons stand for a fatal, human self-consciousness?

If these marks are emblematical of Original Sin, their possessors become particularly useful in showing how such a concept can comport with complete innocence as innocence is judged by worldly standards. We do not blame Georgiana for submitting to the experiment; we do not blame Billy for striking the Master-at-Arms. Original Sin means limitation, a failure somewhere along the line, a lack or shortcoming in no sense criminal, although a criminal act may possibly spring from such a lack or shortcoming, as happened in Billy's case.

At the same time, both stories seem to convey the idea that human perfection is not for this world. At the moment when the crimson hand entirely disappeared from Georgi-

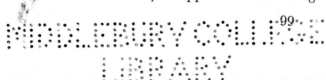

ana's cheek, she died, being translated, as it were, to a heaven where perfection is at home. And, similarly, when Billy, the trap about to be sprung, and the moment of "translation" being at hand, called out "God bless Captain Vere," he spoke the words without the slightest trace of impediment. There is a hint in both stories, and especially in *Billy Budd,* of an analogy with Christ, whose perfection made Him unsuited to an imperfect world. Melville's eloquent account of Billy's last moments carries overtones of Christ's death and ascension:

Billy stood facing aft. At the penultimate moment, his words, his only ones, words wholly unobstructed in the utterance were these—"God bless Captain Vere"! . . . syllables delivered in the clear melody of a singing-bird on the point of launching from the twig. . . . At the same moment, it chanced that the vapory fleece, hanging low in the East, was shot through with a soft glory as of the fleece of the Lamb of God seen in mystical vision, and simultaneously therewith, watched by the wedged mass of upturned faces, Billy ascended; and, ascending, took the full rose of the dawn.

If Billy is "innocence," though not "perfection," Claggart is depravity of the blackest sort. How to account for Claggart's depravity? Melville calls it "natural depravity, a depravity according to nature." He also calls such depravity a "mystery," and quotes St. Paul on "the mystery of iniquity." How to account for Claggart's antipathy to Billy? Again, an unfathomable mystery. "For what," asks Melville, "can more partake of the mysterious than an antipathy spontaneous and profound such as is evoked in certain exceptional mortals by the mere aspect of some other mortal, however harmless he may be? if not called forth by this very harmlessness itself?" Shakespeare dealt with a somewhat similar question in the motivation of Iago. Coleridge said that Iago's villainy came from "a motiveless malignity." Iago said of Cassio, "He hath a daily

beauty in his life/ That makes me ugly." Possibly Claggart felt shamed by Billy's innocence and beauty.

Captain Vere was confident that Billy was not guilty of Claggart's charge of fomenting mutiny, and felt that the fatal blow struck by Billy was an act of divine justice: "It is the divine judgment of Ananias," he said; "Struck dead by an angel of God." And he added, ironically, "Yet the angel must hang!" For the Captain was the custodian of the law, and the law must be enforced. Billy will certainly be acquitted, he believed, "at the last assizes," but "here," he said, "we must proceed under the law of the Mutiny Act." Captain Vere is sympathetically drawn. He is a practical man, making such compromises as he must, in an imperfect world, between the theoretically desirable and the practically attainable.

Claggart is unrelieved evil, and is destroyed, for though the world contains much evil, the good principle strives against it (A.C. Bradley once made this point about *King Lear*),[3] and often succeeds in expelling embodiments of total evil, like Claggart. But just as that evil ship, the *Pequod,* the skyhawk's wing being nailed to the mast, "would not sink to hell till she had dragged a living part of heaven along with her," so Claggart (though not dragging Billy to *hell* unless perchance to *harry* it) brought to an end the earthly life of Billy Budd.

Do the good and evil forces, then, merely cancel each other out? No, there is a residue of good. There is the memory of Billy. The sailors revered Billy's memory. To them a chip of the spar from which he was hanged "was as a piece of the Cross." Even Captain Vere reverenced the memory of Billy, the Captain most of all. On his death-bed, he was heard to murmur, "Billy Budd, Billy Budd." It was as if, Billy being a type of Christ, faith in Billy and his atoning death were the power of God unto salvation to everyone that believeth.

[3] *Shakespearean Tragedy* (2d ed., London, 1905), pp. 303–304.

Ahab's last words before he was jerked out of his boat by the harpoon rope were words of defiance. "From hell's heart I stab at thee," he yelled at the White Whale, "for hate's sake I spit my last breath at thee." Forty years later, Melville wrote a story with a different kind of ending. Just as Christ answered "never a word" to the accusations made against him before Pilate, Billy could say nothing against Claggart's charges when brought before Captain Vere. And just as Christ blessed his enemies (*Father forgive them for they know not what they do*), Billy blessed Captain Vere.

Some have regarded *Billy Budd* as Melville's own personal testament of acceptance, and have reasoned that as *Moby Dick* reflects the rebellion of Melville's youth, *Billy Budd* shows the reconcilement of his old age. This view is open to the objection that it identifies rather too closely the author of an imaginative work with his characters, thereby reducing the work to mere autobiography. It is well not to confuse the critical question with the biographical question. At the same time, both Ahab and Billy are portrayed with a good deal of sympathy, and it is reasonable to suppose that each character, in his respective period, reflects something of the mood of his creator. *Billy Budd* certainly is a brilliant and moving statement of the ultimate Christian lesson of resignation to God's overruling Providence, and it is pleasant, as well as reasonable, to think that Melville in his last years felt the truth of this view. Perhaps he couldn't have written a book like *Billy Budd* without feeling it.

Although James was a very different kind of writer from Melville, he, too, shows the influence of Hawthorne, for like Hawthorne, he was concerned with the loss of innocence, and the snares of a refined egotism.

Many of James's protagonists are learners; they begin comparatively innocent, and end comparatively wise. It is a variation on the theme of the fortunate fall. Many of James's characters are "innocent" Americans who travel to Europe, where their experiences have a maturing effect. America in many of his stories is a symbol of "innocence"; Europe, a symbol of "knowledge." If Isabel Archer, a charming young lady from Albany, New York (in *Portrait of a Lady*), is less happy after several months' residence in Europe, and her marriage to Gilbert Osmond, she has tasted of the tree of knowledge, she is a wiser and deeper person. One grows through suffering. Expulsion from the Garden is necessary to human development. An even richer instance is that of Lambert Strether, a New Englander (in *The Ambassadors*), who was exposed to the "evil" of a Parisian society, and, though shocked, profited from the exposure. Unlike Hawthorne's Goodman Brown, whose traumatic experience proved utterly blighting, Strether throve, and, one might say, grew in grace and knowledge. He threw off some of the old bigotry; he grew in charity and understanding; he became a humane person.

Not that James denies the evil. Although evil in James may seem not evil at all, it is so refined, it contains so little grossness, it is evil still. The liaison of Madame de Vionnet (that most charming of heroines) and Chad Newsome is not a "virtuous" relationship, and the book doesn't mean to say that it is. The book does mean to say that so far as Madame de Vionnet and Strether are concerned (Chad proves to be a cad, and doesn't count), the evil is overcome with good. In a memorable scene, Madame de Vionnet sat one morning in Notre Dame in a rapt, concentrated mood, which the reader takes to be the finest essence of religious devotion, and although Strether is not a Catholic, he manages to catch something of her mood of acquiescence. These wonderfully fine people, after their respective ordeals, meet finally and briefly (for James here, as in so many places, insists upon the virtue of renunciation) on an exalted plane of mutual appreciation.

The insidiousness of egotism was James's great concern, as it was Hawthorne's. Hawthorne's tale, "Egotism, or the Bosom Serpent," used a snake as a symbol of self-involvement, and the chief character in that story goes about crying "It gnaws me, it gnaws me!" Gilbert Osmond, the villain of *Portrait of a Lady,* does nothing so melodramatic as that, but James (remembering Hawthorne's tale, very likely) says of him, "His egotism lay hidden like a serpent in a bank of flowers." Osmond (like Aylmer in "The Birthmark") tried to remake his young wife, Isabel, after his own notion of excellence. Perhaps the wonder and charm of Strether and Madame de Vionnet are owing to the fact that they both had become so little the egotists. They both, in their genuine concern for others, had exorcised, or, if that is never quite possible, reduced to a decently limited status, the bosom serpent. They both had become selfless, or almost so.

Perhaps the most impressive example in James's fiction of a man who could not become selfless, until it was too late, is John Marcher, in *The Beast in the Jungle.* Here is a man who got the vain idea that something very special was going to happen to him, something which would distinguish him notably from all other men. This was a sin of presumption, to begin with. Having got such an idea, he set himself to watching and waiting, with mingled hope and fear. He confided his obsession to a lovely woman, May Bartram, and she agreed to join him in his vigil. May, of course, was in love with Marcher, while Marcher was in love only with himself. Even in the company of the lady, he had thoughts only for his own special fate. Self, Self, Self—Ego, Ego, Ego—filled his consciousness.

James dramatizes the story in two powerful scenes. In one, May, frail and mortally ill after many years of fruitless waiting, yet still beautiful in her slender, pale way, enters the fireless parlor on a chilly afternoon in April (April is the cruellest month), and tottering, wavering, before Marcher, virtually offers herself to him. But he is impervious, unaware—so self-involved he continues to be. It is Marcher's last chance, and he passes it by.

The other scene of great dramatic power comes at the end. It is a scene of self-revelation: Marcher comes to himself, he sees himself for the monster of egotism that he is, but it is too late. While visiting May's grave, he is struck by the face of another visitor in the cemetery, a man who is mourning for his lost love. The other man's face is ravaged with grief, and Marcher, seeing the face, realizes "the way a woman is mourned when she has been loved for herself." Marcher learns, at last, what his exceptional, tragic fate is: "He has been the man of his time, *the* man, to whom nothing on earth was to have happened. That was the rare stroke—that was his visitation."

The concluding pages of *The Beast in the Jungle* are so extraordinarily explicit and powerful (they are, I think, the most explicit and powerful direct statement in James's entire works) that part of the passage must be quoted:

The stranger passed, but the raw glare of his grief remained, making our friend wonder in pity what wrong, what wound it expressed, what injury not to be healed. What had the man *had,* to make him, by the loss of it, so bleed and yet live?

Something—and this reached him with a pang—that *he,* John Marcher, hadn't; the proof of which was precisely John Marcher's arid end. No passion had ever touched him, for this was what passion meant; he had survived and maundered and pined, but where had been *his* deep ravage? The extraordinary thing we speak of was the sudden rush of the result of this question. The sight that had just met his eyes named to him, as in letters of quick flame, something he had utterly, insanely missed, and what he had missed made these things a train of fire, made them mark themselves in an anguish of inward throbs. He had seen *outside* of his life, not learned it within, the way a woman was mourned when she had been loved for herself; such was the force of his conviction of the meaning of the stranger's face, which still flared for him like a smoky torch. . . .

The escape would have been to love her; then, *then* he

would have lived. *She* had lived—who could say now with what passion?—since she had loved him for himself; whereas he had never thought of her but in the chill of his egotism and the light of her use. . . . He saw the Jungle of his life and saw the lurking Beast; then, while he looked, perceived it, as by a stir of the air, rise, huge and hideous, for the leap that was to settle him. His eyes darkened—it was close; and, instinctively turning, in his hallucination, to avoid it, he flung himself, on his face, on the tomb.

Marcher is overwhelmed, and destroyed, by the realization of his monstrous egotism, of which the Beast is symbol.

Where had been *his* deep ravage? James joins Dickinson ("I like a look of agony") and Hawthorne ("Have we not ransomed each other with all this woe?") in his emphasis upon the necessity of suffering. It is the meaning of the Christian Cross, and it is worth recalling that James used a cross—a fine Maltese cross, an *objet d'art*—as the key symbol of another great story of his, *The Spoils of Poynton*, where the suffering was, appropriately, of a particularly excruciating kind.

I call Hawthorne, Melville, and James "counter-romantics" because they recognize Original Sin, because they show the conflict between good and evil, because they show man's struggle toward redemption, because they dramatize the necessary role of suffering in the purification of the self. They do not apotheosize the self, as romantics like Emerson and Whitman do, but warn against its perversities, its obsessions, its insidious deceptions. They side with the orthodox, traditional Christian view of man and the world. It is an interesting sidelight on the moral temper of our time that the three writers considered in this chapter are regarded today, with almost complete critical unanimity, as the greatest American writers of the nineteenth century.

V ✳ *The Amoralists*

"NATURALISM" in the modern novel is based upon "scientific determinism." Man, according to this view, is a product of forces over which he has no control. The forces may be biological or social; they may belong to one's heredity or one's environment. In any case, they reduce man to the status of a puppet. If man is a puppet, he is clearly not a moral agent, he is relieved of moral responsibility, he deserves neither blame nor praise, he is always doing the best—or the worst—he can. Amoralism is an inevitable corollary of naturalism.

I suggested in an earlier chapter the paradoxical difference between scientific determinism and the determinism (though the word, I think, should not be used in a religious context) implied in an Overruling Providence: the former concept is destructive of the moral responsibility of the individual, while the latter is not. Acquiescence in the Divine Decrees leaves man still obligated to exert himself to the limit, to do his utmost. If it is true that the harder he works, the more difficult acquiescence may be when the outcome is at variance with his aims (as it is likely to be more often than not), why then, this is one of the tests a Christian must learn to meet. A Christian must be able to say "The judgments of the Lord are true and righteous altogether," and keep on trying. Scientific determinism has a quite different import and effect.

There is a real danger that much of the "testing" which is going on now, especially in the colleges, may have the bad effect of minimizing individual responsibility by giving the individual the impression that there are certain things which he *can't* do, and would be foolish to attempt. Our college advisory system would never permit Demosthenes to "major" in oratory: he had a speech impediment. But he overcame the impediment by practising speaking with a pebble in his mouth, and became the greatest orator of the ancient world. Our college advisors should read more biography. If they did, they would see how often men with great handicaps have become great; in fact, true greatness seems nearly always to have been predicated on an apparently insuperable difficulty to be overcome.

Modern scientific determinism becomes more insidious all the while. Poverty breeds crime, say some. But how many of us have sprung from "poor but honest parents"? The phrase is, in fact, or used to be, a cliché of biography. A glandular determinism is popular with many. "If the thyroid doesn't get you," they say, "then the pituitary must." The psychiatric patient feels that his emotional disturbance has got him licked, and it becomes the job of the psychiatrist to convince him that it hasn't. This is, or has been in times past, the office of religion. St. Paul said, "I can do all things through Christ," which is a little different from our modern naturalistic version, "I can do only those things which my psychological profile shows that I have an aptitude for, and I should be silly to try anything else."

Naturalism in literature began with the powerful novels of Émile Zola. Consider *Germinal,* for example. Here we have the story of the coal miners in northern France. Their lot is a wretched one. The author piles up such a tremendous mass of facts (or "documentation"), that the reader becomes thoroughly acquainted with the subject, and feels as if he had actually shared the life described. There *is,* one is almost constrained to feel after having read *Germinal,* a connection between poverty and crime.

The subject matter and method of the naturalistic novel

derive from its philosophy. Modern industry is often used (the coal industry is used in *Germinal*) because the industrial worker (in Zola's time) seemed comparatively helpless. Social and economic facts are piled up, because the author's aim is to show the overwhelming force of circumstance. "Little people" are often preferred, because they *appear* (of course they aren't, necessarily) more amenable to the forces. "Low life" is often presented because relaxed standards are more suitable to the author's purpose. Zola gave his fiction an aura of science. He spoke of the "experimental novel," as if the writing of fiction were a kind of scientific experiment. Given certain people, living under certain conditions, how will they act? Zola thought of the craft of the novel as a controlled experiment, and of people as elements in a chemical reaction.

American novelists of the 1890's like Stephen Crane and Frank Norris were influenced by Zola's naturalism. The effect in general was to reduce the stature of the individual, and to deprive him of autonomy and responsibility. Naturalism, here, is at the opposite pole from romanticism. If romantics like Emerson and Whitman exalted man to the level of the Deity, so that he became in Emerson's phrase "part and parcel of God," naturalists like Zola and his American disciples reduced man to the level of helplessness and ineffectualness.

Crane's *Maggie, A Girl of the Streets* showed the immoral effects on an innately nice girl of bad surroundings, in this case, the Bowery in New York City. In *The Red Badge of Courage,* the same author showed the confusions and fears of the private soldier. Like soldiers in more modern war novels, he is pushed around by the war. If Crane's soldier achieves a certain moral stature toward the end, the author, to that extent, stops short of being a complete naturalist. Crane's fine story *The Open Boat* emphasizes the immensity of the Universe, and man's littleness in comparison. It was perhaps the first important American story to show man against the backdrop of the new universe of modern science.

As the four shipwrecked men take their turns at the oars, and as they become progressively weary during the long night, they look up occasionally at the starry heavens, and looking up, they are impressed chiefly by the stars' remoteness and indifference. Their thoughts are described in the following passage:

> When it occurs to a man that nature does not regard him as important, and that she feels she would not maim the universe by disposing of him, he at first wishes to throw bricks at the temple, and he hates deeply the fact that there are no bricks and no temples. Any visible expression of nature would surely be pelleted with his jeers.
>
> Then, if there be no tangible thing to hoot, he feels, perhaps, the desire to confront a personification and indulge in pleas, bowed to one knee, and with hands supplicant, saying, "Yes, but I love myself."
>
> A high cold star on a winter's night is the word he feels that she says to him. Thereafter he knows the pathos of his situation.

A high cold star on a winter's night! The star is both high (remote) and cold (indifferent). The universe is very large, and man is only a tiny speck in it. Astronomically speaking, man is insignificant. Actually, of course, this immense and indifferent universe is man's discovery, and so it would seem truer (as well as more flattering) to say, Astronomically speaking, man is the astronomer! But the impression persists and will not down (it is one of the ironies of modern intellectual history) that man has been dwarfed by his own discovery. He has been dwarfed by his universe because of its size, and estranged from it because of its coldness. Tom Paine could hardly have foreseen such an outcome when he recommended the study of the "Bible of Creation."

There is, then, a naturalistic theme in Crane. Man is overwhelmed, or in danger of being overwhelmed, by the forces: the mass movements of war, the immoral life of the slums, the elemental forces of the universe itself. Frank Norris also gave a large emphasis to the importance of external forces in determining man's life on this planet. In *The Octopus* and *The Pit* he shows the power of wheat, first, on the farms of California, where it is grown, and second, in the Chicago Board of Trade, where it is bought and sold. To Norris, the contrast between the individual person and the forces generated and let loose by the wheat underscored man's puniness. He wrote in *The Octopus:*

As if human agency could affect this colossal power! What were these heated, tiny squabbles, this feverish, small bustle of mankind, this minute swarming of the human insect, to the great, majestic, silent ocean of the Wheat itself! Indifferent, gigantic, resistless, it moved in its appointed grooves. Men, Lilliputians, gnats in the sunshine, buzzed impudently in their tiny battles, were born, lived through their little day, died, and were forgotten; while the Wheat, wrapped in Nirvanic calm, grew steadily under the night, alone with the stars and with God.

To the naturalist, man is "the human insect"; nature and nature's "God" are alike contemptuous of such a "gnat." To the Psalmist, who considered the same question, man was not rendered insignificant by his physical surroundings. The following passage implies that man is more important than the material creation:

When I consider thy heavens, the work of thy fingers, the moon and the stars, which thou hast ordained; what is man that thou art mindful of him? and the son of man, that thou visitest him? For thou hast made him a little lower than the angels, and hast crowned him with glory and honor. Thou madest him to have dominion over the works of thy hands; thou hast put all things under his feet: All sheep and oxen, yea, and the beasts of the field; the fowl of the air, and the fish of the sea, and whatsoever passeth through the paths of the seas. O Lord our Lord, how excellent is thy name in all the earth!

One mistake of naturalists like Crane and Norris was to put man too low in the scale of creation. It is not surprising, because their philosophy was a materialistic one, and in such a philosophy, the criterion of importance may well be the amount of mere mass or force. The Psalmist is not so misled. He knows that man is only a *little* lower than the angels. The two passages show rather well the difference between the materialistic and the religious views of life.

Norris went farther than Crane, in one direction, in the exploration of naturalism. In his novel *McTeague* he discovered and unleashed a powerful "force" from within the chief character himself. This force is animalism or animal instinct. McTeague is an animal-like brute who knows only how to use his physical strength to get what he wants. He is sluggish and harmless so long as he is well-fed and undisturbed, but when crossed or thwarted, he resorts to his fists. He kills his wife, and flees to the Great Desert, where he is captured by his former friend, now his enemy. He kills his enemy, only to find himself manacled to him, in the middle of Death Valley. Society is not at all to blame for McTeague's actions, nor, according to Norris, is McTeague himself. Men, Norris says, are sometimes ruled by Master Passions, and men like McTeague are helpless when seized by the primal urge, the abysmal brutish animalism.

In the naturalistic view, then, man is ruled by forces from without or forces from within, or both. Some novels stress environment more than heredity (for example, Crane's *Maggie*), and some stress heredity more than environment (for example, Norris' *McTeague*). Some novels emphasize the two nearly equally. Social and economic conditions are very important in Theodore Dreiser's *An American Tragedy*, for example, but so is heredity or temperament.

Being a puppet of the forces, man can hardly appear in a heroic light, and it is a question whether the term "hero" can properly be applied to the protagonist, or chief actor, in a work of naturalistic fiction. The term "hero" suggests a morally responsible actor, and suggests, too, that certain adverse forces are being overcome by wilful endeavor. The heroic actor becomes himself a force to be reckoned with. If the conflict is internal, then his better nature is capable of asserting itself, and often does assert itself.

If terms like "heroic" and "hero" are applicable to a given story, the work can hardly be regarded as compatible with the philosophy of naturalism. If the soldier in *The Red Badge of Courage* becomes a hero at the end (and he seems to emerge as something of a hero; he has acquired a quiet self-confidence, and he leads a successful charge), Crane has transcended, at that point, the limitations imposed by naturalism. A similar qualification, I think, must be made concerning Norris' wheat novels, where courageous, responsible action by certain individuals is sometimes displayed. For this reason, Crane and Norris, I believe, were not complete naturalists. They were much impressed by new concepts of force supplied by the modern natural and social sciences. They felt that these new concepts had a bearing on the question of moral responsibility, and that man, in the light of them, became less responsible, and particularly less blameworthy for his misdeeds and failings. But they were unwilling to give up completely the concept of the hero and the heroic in human history. They wound up by being not much more than halfway naturalists.

The naturalistic novelist who perhaps came nearer than any other American writer of stature to going the whole way was Theodore Dreiser, and the novel which I think best exemplifies this statement is his *An American Tragedy*, published in 1925. If I seem to give a disproportionate amount of space to this work, it is partly because I think *An American Tragedy* is an impressive book, and partly because it is probably the most completely naturalistic of all American novels. It can therefore be very useful as a norm and touchstone, especially in view of the fact that the term "naturalistic" has been attached, I believe, to a number of American books to which it properly belongs, either not at all, or only in a very qualified sense.

This is the story of Clyde Griffiths. It begins when he is twelve, and ends ten years later, when Clyde, at the age of twenty-two, is sent to the electric chair for the murder of Roberta Alden. It is told in three parts.

The story begins with a Salvation Army meeting conducted by Clyde's parents on a street corner in Kansas City. Clyde views the proceedings with distaste. His father is the weak, ineffectual sort; his mother, though resolute, has a mediocre mind. The older daughter, who plays the organ, later runs away with an actor, and still later, returns pregnant and unmarried. Clyde, when he is seventeen, gets a job in a big downtown hotel, where he is initiated into the life of the bellhop world. The bellhops have money to spend: tips run from four to six dollars a day. Clyde goes with the others on a drinking party, and afterwards to a whore house. (Dreiser describes these things always factually and patiently, and never salaciously.) The bellhops take their girl friends out into the country one afternoon in a borrowed car. On the way back, the car strikes a child, and the panicky driver speeds the car into the suburbs, and wrecks it in an open field. At the end of Part I Clyde is crawling on all fours across a snow-covered field in the semidarkness.

It might be well to pause at this point to attempt a preliminary assessment of Clyde and his situation. He was underprivileged. He had almost no schooling, though he was bright enough. He adopted the mores of his set, the bellhop set. He was very adaptable, quick to learn; he quickly took on the coloration of the group in which he found himself. He was in no way to blame for the accident, and he did not run away from the scene of the accident—the driver did that. But he ran away from the crack-up in the field, and was never seen again in those parts. He was weak. His early religious training is not supposed to have been of any particular use to him. "Successful" people look down on street preachers. Clyde wanted to be a "success" like the rich people he saw at the big hotel. He was ambitious; he wanted to rise in the scale. He aspired to the "higher things" of his materialistic environment: money, clothes, good times, sexual excitement. Is a young man very much to blame, Dreiser asks in effect, for embracing the "ideals" of his surroundings, the "ideals" which on all sides stare him brazenly in the face?

Clyde's father's brother, Samuel Griffiths, is a successful manufacturer of shirts and collars in Lycurgus, upstate New York, and Part II begins with an account of the Lycurgus Griffiths and their circle. What a rich luxurious picture, what an impressive picture, the author paints of life on fashionable Wykeagy Avenue! The fine houses in Renaissance style, excellent period copies of French, Italian, and English models; the alert, businesslike Samuel Griffiths and his rising son Gilbert, Princeton graduate and secretary of the firm; the fashionable and lively young ladies, Bella Griffiths and her bosom friends Bertine Cranston (of the Cranston Wickwire Company) and Sondra Finchley (of the equally important Finchley Electric Sweeper), all enrolled in the select Snedeker School; the parties, the gaiety, the snobbery—how different all this from Clyde's world!

Clyde hopped on a box car after we last saw him, and eventually reached Chicago, and got a job at the Union League. Here he saw Samuel Griffiths, in Chicago on business, and introduced himself. His uncle offered him a job, and Clyde went at once to Lycurgus, and was given, by cousin Gilbert, a menial assignment in the Shrinking Department at fifteen dollars a week. Some time later, he was promoted to the headship of the Collar Stamping Department, where he became interested in Roberta Alden, an unsophisticated girl from the country. After he had become involved with Roberta, he was taken up by the Wykeagy set, and found that he could not resist the attractions of high society. He became infatuated with Sondra Finchley, and she with him. And so, Clyde faced a great problem. Roberta was with child, but Clyde aspired to Sondra, the rich society belle. Roberta would not release him, and Clyde was unwilling to give up Sondra. What a quandary for a young man to find himself in, who is, so far as the reader can discover, utterly without character!

Dreiser's portrait is sympathetically drawn, nevertheless, and the reader is perforce sympathetically disposed, too, so compelling are the forces, and so ill-prepared is Clyde to cope with them. Dreiser's depiction of Clyde's quandary is surely a masterpiece of American realism: the talk with the druggist, the visit to the country doctor, his writing to Ratterer, his old K.C. pal, Roberta's ignorance of sex, Clyde's ignorance too, the whole social attitude toward the unmarried mother, Clyde's shallow infatuation with a girl of much less real worth than Roberta—all this adds up to what is perhaps the most convincing "slice of life" to be found anywhere in the American novel.

Clyde plotted Roberta's murder. The growth of this idea, the germ of which came from a newspaper story, is plausibly traced. At length, he attempted to carry out the plot, but the circumstances were somewhat equivocal. When he and Roberta were in the boat in the middle of the lake, he became so distraught that Roberta, supposing him ill, moved in his direction, and he, holding a camera in his hand and making an involuntary gesture, struck her with the camera and overturned the boat; whereupon Clyde, a good swimmer, permitted Roberta, who couldn't swim, to drown.

At the end of Part II we see Clyde hurrying away from the lake through the darkening forest in the direction of the Finchley's summer lodge. We remember that at the end of Part I the young man was running away, or crawling away, in the semidarkness. At that time, he was not to blame for what had happened, and the reader suspects that the author would like to imply that Clyde is again an unfortunate victim of circumstances.

Part III, the last part, begins with a detailed account of the legal machinery by which Clyde was to be tried. Much information is given about the District Attorney, to show how and why he was unsympathetically disposed toward Clyde. Much information is given also about Clyde's lawyers, their personal histories, their quirks. The power of the press is emphasized, and the power of local politics and local prejudices. Clyde, of course, is at the mercy of these external forces, seems in fact helpless in the face of them. His lawyers concoct an untrue story because they think it will be more readily believed than Clyde's somewhat truer story—truth is stranger than fiction, they say—and they drill Clyde in their version.

Toward the end of the trial, Clyde's mother comes to the prison to pray with Clyde. After the verdict of guilty in the first degree, she writes pieces for the paper and gives public lectures on Clyde's history, to get money to pay for a new trial—which is never granted. A young minister, the Reverend Mr. McMillan, takes a great interest in Clyde. He writes a statement, and persuades Clyde to sign it, in which Clyde warns young men against sinful ways, and professes to have found the peace of God. Part III ends with Clyde's death in the electric chair. In an epilogue, the book ends as it began: Clyde's parents, older and feebler, are conducting a Salvation Army meeting on a street corner in San Francisco.

Malcolm Cowley has made the observation that the American naturalists (they were mostly newspaper men) believed that "Christianity was a sham." [1] The statement seems to fit Dreiser pretty well.

I imagine Dreiser thought he was giving Christianity a thorough and fair trial in *An American Tragedy,* that he was weighing it in the balance and finding it wanting. However underprivileged Clyde may have been, he at least had a Christian upbringing. This, however, did not save him from crime. Nor did Christianity bring him comfort in his last days. He had not found peace, as his ghostwriter said he had. He ended wretchedly. McMillan himself, moreover, was a phony. He knew that the statement was untrue. He wanted to use Clyde to advance his own professional interests, he wanted to be known as a great soul-saver.

That leaves Clyde's mother to be accounted for. Dreiser could hardly denigrate her Christian character. He may not have known it, but she was a saint, and the Christian reader knows she was a saint. The Christian reader knows also that her great strength and endurance came from her religious faith. Well, even if Dreiser will allow this, his attitude toward her is still one, not of admiration, but pity; and pity not so much because of the unhappiness inflicted upon her by a wayward son, as because of her failure to follow a more "profitable" course in life. She was not brilliant, to be sure, but she had a certain practical talent. Her lecturing and work for the newspaper showed she could make money—she made over a thousand dollars, in a fairly short time. Why did she keep on with her street preaching

[1] "A Natural History of American Naturalism," reprinted in *Critiques and Essays on Modern Fiction,* ed. John W. Aldridge (New York, 1952).

and mission work? What did she get out of it? the author seems to ask, incredulous, bewildered. She was—Dreiser believes, and would have us believe—a poor, misguided creature.

Our author is, I fear, spiritually benighted. He is addicted to the same materialism of which poor Clyde is the bounden slave. One has only to compare Dreiser's treatment of Clyde's mother with Faulkner's treatment of Dilsey, in *The Sound and the Fury,* to see the difference—and it is an abysmal one—between the naturalistic and the religious attitudes.

An American Tragedy illustrates perfectly the complete amoralism of the naturalistic philosophy. Clyde Griffiths was not responsible, he was not to blame. Before you judge Clyde, Dreiser says in effect, don't forget the child's uneasiness at those sidewalk meetings; the accident on the way back from the bellhop party; the shabby treatment he received from the Lycurgus Griffiths; his excitable sexual nature; his dreams of wealth and position (stemming—did they not?—from the respectable current American materialism); his innate weakness. One of Clyde's lawyers, in a speech before the court, called his client "a mental and moral coward," and added, "You didn't make yourself, did you, Clyde?" Clyde is not responsible, in the last analysis, because he didn't make himself. And this, I fear, is the gospel according to Theodore Dreiser.

Dreiser is the most compassionate of writers. Sherwood Anderson in a sensitive little sketch (in his *Horses and Men*) tells a story of Dreiser's sitting on the platform at an orphan asylum, watching the children trooping in, in their neat uniforms. "The tears ran down his cheeks," Anderson said, "and he folded and refolded his pocket handkerchief, and shook his head." The picture is revealing, and appealing. Dreiser, when confronted by human troubles, is overwhelmed by pity and perplexity. He doesn't know what to do with life. The tears run down his cheeks, and he folds and refolds his pocket handkerchief, and shakes his head.

Compassion is a great virtue, but it is not necessary to surrender individual responsibility in order to be compassionate. There is such a thing as Christian forgiveness and Christian pity. Jesus was compassionate toward the thief on the cross, and the woman taken in adultery. *The Scarlet Letter* is compassionate, without surrendering the responsible individual. "There but for the grace of God go I" is a better basis for compassion than the general denial of responsibility.

Our best naturalist next to Dreiser is, I think, James T. Farrell. In *Young Lonigan,* we see the inexorable shaping effect of Chicago's South Side on an adolescent boy. Studs Lonigan belongs to a gang, and he does what the gang does. He is not a "weakling" like Clyde; he is even something of a leader; but his life is shaped none the less by the mores of the community. The mores are low, and the result is low. Home and school and church are entirely ineffectual in counteracting the lowness. There is a touch of ideality at one point when Studs and a nice girl sit in a tree in the park, but this touch is easily effaced (too easily? one may ask) by the influence of another kind of girl. Not once does Studs transcend the environment. Not once does he show self-discipline, or moral courage, or a sense of duty, or any of the ideal traits. If one wishes another touchstone (I have already offered one or two) by which to measure the difference between the naturalistic view and the anti-naturalistic, or humanistic, or Christian, one can compare Studs with another famous American boy, Huckleberry Finn.[2]

Mark Twain put forth comparatively late in life a naturalistic argument in an essay called "What is Man?" But

[2] Or Hemingway's Nick Adams, in *In Our Time.*

the argument had already been refuted to the satisfaction of most of his readers in *The Adventures of Huckleberry Finn*. Mark Twain could never be classed among the naturalists if for no other reason than the fact that Huck is one of the most responsible of fictional mortals. When he tore up the letter to Miss Watson telling of Jim's whereabouts, and thus set himself squarely against the mores of the slaveholding community where he had grown up, he made a moral choice of the first magnitude. He proved that the social environment is not necessarily all-powerful in shaping one's acts. He showed that the individual will—what Lionel Trilling has called "the opposing self"—can generate a force of its own, which is capable of competing with other "deterministic" forces, and perchance, on a lucky occasion, of overcoming them. Huck's grim "All right then, I'll go to hell!" is one of the most powerful antinaturalistic ✓ declarations in all literature.

I am inclined to think that we do not find as much naturalism in American literature as some have supposed; that the term "naturalism" has been used a bit loosely on occasion; that, while we may have produced, say, a half-dozen good solid naturalists, many of our writers who have been called "naturalistic" were not really so. I am inclined to believe that the naturalistic philosophy has proved uncongenial, in the main, to the American temperament.

One would expect to find that the "muckrakers" of the early 1900's were thoroughgoing naturalists. Their aim was to expose abuses in our economic and social life. Two famous examples (there are many others) are Upton Sinclair's *The Jungle* published in 1906, and David Graham Phillips' *Susan Lenox,* published in 1915. Sinclair showed the meatpacking establishment in Chicago to be a horribly bad place to work, and Phillips exposed the assorted immoralities of New York City. In both books the emphasis is on "conditions." Environment becomes an all-powerful force. But the authors are unwilling to allow the force of environment, as great as it is, to overwhelm their protagonists.

Jurgis, the young Lithuanian immigrant, is beaten down by the stockyards, but he emerges at the end buoyed up by a new faith, a faith in "socialism." The full title of Phillips' novel is *Susan Lenox, Her Fall and Rise.* We are told that Susan kept her self-respect despite her degraded life (she was a prostitute, among other things). She had an abnormally strong heart; and she read Emerson, who helped her to lead a life of the mind and spirit apart from the repulsive physical reality surrounding her. I mention these two examples by way of suggesting the point that even the muckrakers, who were perhaps more deeply committed to the environmental theory than any other group of novelists, liked to show the triumph of the individual spirit over the most sordid surroundings. Their protagonists do, on occasion, take on heroic proportions, and in so far as this is true, the term "naturalistic" seems not to apply.

One sometimes sees Sinclair Lewis called a naturalist, but in his great books, written in the 1920's, his protagonists can tower, heroically, above their surroundings. Dr. Martin Arrowsmith is a first-class hero; he accomplishes great things in the medical world against enormous odds. Despite her foolishness and impracticality, Carol Kennicott is entitled to our respect. Her speech to Dr. Will at the end of *Main Street* is still impressive: ". . . this Community Day makes me see how thoroughly I'm beaten. . . . But I have won in this: I've never excused my failures by sneering at my aspirations, by pretending to have gone beyond them. I do not admit that Main Street is as beautiful as it should be! I do not admit that Gopher Prairie is greater or more generous than Europe! I do not admit that dishwashing is enough to satisfy all women! I may not have fought the good fight, but I have kept the faith."

I like Carol's allusion to St. Paul's "I have fought a good

fight . . . I have kept the faith." Carol had kept the faith, and had fought a good fight, too. One other example of a good fighter in Lewis' fiction must be mentioned: Sam Dodsworth, who achieved spiritual independence by winning a hard-fought victory over the great American vice —personified in his wife, Fran—of keeping up with the Joneses. The term "naturalistic" is not applicable to characters and books like these.

I should not want to call Thomas Wolfe a naturalist merely because he goes in for facts and notations, and sordid details (the classifiers are sometimes misled by superficial aspects of the naturalistic or Zolaesque novel). Eugene Gant—that towering passionate giant of the Carolina mountains—is not a recognizable child of naturalism. If the environment sometimes oppresses him, if his heredity sometimes seems a handicap, we feel at work, nevertheless, a sufficiently formidable "opposing self."

Hemingway and Faulkner have been called "naturalists" by certain classifiers, who decided long ago that the twentieth century is *The Naturalistic Period*. An attempt will be made in the next chapter to consider Hemingway and Faulkner. It will suffice here to make one or two observations.

The fact that we have come almost unconsciously to speak of "the Hemingway hero" is in itself significant. If he *is* a hero, his conduct must be, in part at least, heroic. Such conduct exalts man, and does not fit the concept of naturalism which this chapter has tried to establish. Although the corresponding expression, "the Faulkner hero," may not be so current, Faulkner is even less of a naturalist than Hemingway. Faulkner's books, John Crowe Ransom has said, show us man "under the aspect of magnificence." Many of his characters tower; they increase our notion of the human potential. Faulkner, moreover, is seriously concerned with "sin," and there is no "sin" in naturalism.

Naturalism and romanticism commit the same error,

though for different reasons, of denying sin. There is no
sin in romanticism because man is not a sinner. He is innately good, infinitely perfectible, and potentially, when
not actually, God. Romanticism (the reader will recall that
I am taking Emerson as norm) narrows the gap separating
man and God to the vanishing point. Naturalism makes a
similar error, at the opposite end of the scale. It narrows
to the vanishing point the gap separating man and the
animals. There is no sin because there is no moral nature.
There is no choice, no responsibility, no fault.

One literary result common to romanticism and naturalism is the absence of tragedy in the high sense. Allen Tate
pointed out (in the *locus* already cited) that there is no
tragic possibility in Emerson's scheme because there can
be no conflict in Emerson's monistic world. Well, the
naturalistic world of Dreiser is equally monistic, and
equally incompatible with tragedy. Tragedy requires a
responsible actor who must choose between good and
evil. Clyde Griffiths' case is pathetic rather than truly tragic,
and Dreiser's use of the word "Tragedy" in the title is jour-
nalistic, not literary.

√ Naturalism in American fiction is now about as dead
as the Dodo. However persistent the deterministic-ergo-
amoral approach may be in the realm of the social sciences
(and I am not at all competent to express an opinion here),
the naturalistic view, best represented in our imaginative
literature by Theodore Dreiser, was supplanted quite some
time ago by a kind of neo-orthodoxy, thanks largely to the
literary leadership of the South. For in the South, where
the naturalistic idea had never really taken hold because
the doctrine of Original Sin had never been lost sight of,
giants in prose fiction like William Faulkner and Robert
Penn Warren have been concerned with an order of characters who bear little resemblance to Clyde Griffiths, and a
world of accountability quite unlike Dreiser's amoral

world. Hightower, Sutpen, Munn, Stark, and others of their ilk cannot be measured by scientific determinants. In short, the great Southern fiction writers of our time have brought our literature back to the tradition of Hawthorne and Melville, of Milton and Shakespeare.

VI   *   *The Old Cost of the Human Redemption*

THE MODERN CONSERVATIVE movement has come about as a reaction against nineteenth-century liberalism. What was nineteenth-century liberalism? It had several facets.

It was, in part, what Matthew Arnold called "faith in machinery." It was belief in progress. The evolutionary theory seemed to give the assurance that continuous improvement was inevitable. (One recalls Emerson's "Meliorism is the law.") The growth of democracy gave a similar assurance; the spread of the franchise seemed in itself a guarantee of progress. (I remember hearing it argued, when I was a boy in Middle Tennessee early in the century, that if women were given the vote, there would be no more consumption of alcoholic beverages in the United States.) It was believed, too, that the advance of science and technology would bring about a Utopian world. Emerson reflected the progressive spirit when he said, late in life, that if he were a young man, he would enroll in the college with the best courses in science and engineering. Whitman went along with this view when he exclaimed, in "Song of Myself," "Hurrah for positive science!"

It was believed that the set-up was foolproof, it couldn't fail. Add to all this the belief that man is innately good, and sin only a name, and you have a fair picture of the liberal

126

milieu. Since this milieu was so pervasive and so dominant in the nineteenth century and after, it is no wonder that the sequence of world events dating from August, 1914, produced a good deal of acute pain. For there is no disillusionment quite so painful as that of a disillusioned liberal. The "lost generation" of the 1920's were the unprepared and unwarned inheritors of a progressivism which had backfired in their faces.

William Ellery Channing, one of the great early liberals, declared in 1820 that "Calvinism is giving place to better views." It gave place to more benign, more flattering views, but whether they were better views is open to serious doubt. We are concerned here, of course (as we have been concerned throughout this discussion) with the most fundamental of all questions, *What is the nature of man?* A corollary to this question might be, What have we a right to expect? The view which asserts man's intrinsic goodness, denies Original Sin, effaces the Cross from the human horizon, may be supposed to be an inadequate preparation for "life" in any age. The opposition between Hawthorne and Emerson continues to be of use. Hawthorne was saddened by the American Civil War, but he was not disillusioned by it. Emerson's reaction to the War (the War being so out of keeping with his metaphysical calculations) was the rather insane one of prescribing a policy more extreme even than that of the extreme Reconstructionists.[1] The mental state of the "liberal" who discovers that the world is imperfect, and is likely to continue so for a long time, is not an enviable one. Your Calvinist, on the other hand, may be a bit grim, but he can grin and bear it. He is never too much surprised at the behavior of the *natural* man.

It would be an interesting semantic inquiry to determine to what extent the word "liberal" in a religious context is used favorably today, and to what extent unfavor-

[1] That the slaves themselves be paid in the amount of their market value (See "The Boston Hymn").

ably. A generation or two ago its connotation was certainly favorable in many, perhaps most, quarters; today it is a pejorative in many. Emily Dickinson was probably in a small minority in the Unitarian New England of her day when she satirized the clergyman who preached upon "breadth." Today, she finds a growing number on her side. When Allen Tate named a collection of his pieces, in 1936, *Reactionary Essays,* he was flaunting a sign. Thinking it time for a reaction against a number of impracticable, if not undesirable, progressivisms, he called himself *reactionary,* a word which had been used only in a pejorative sense for a good while. It is still very generally a pejorative, I suppose, so ingrained in America is the progressive idea. "Reactionary" is likely to remain for some time an epithet with which progressives enjoy damning the conservative or orthodox party.

It was used by many progressives no doubt to condemn T.S. Eliot when he announced in the late 1920's that he had become an Anglo-Catholic. A return to the Middle Ages, they said, was an impossible solution. But if we substitute for "Middle Ages" "orthodox Christian belief," wherein is the solution impossible? In the last two or three decades, an increasing number of thoughtful people have sided with Eliot at least to this extent: they believe a return to Christian fundamentals (whether within the Anglo-Catholic fold, or some other) is the chief need of our time. These people (I reject the name "intellectual," used substantively, as by and large an unfortunate usage) are the ones whom I mean to designate as "neo-orthodox." They were probably brought up in the Christian faith, whether Catholic or Protestant. They almost necessarily fell into various kinds of agnosticisms and infidelities. And after having suffered from spiritual famine, like the prodigal son in a far country, they have at length undertaken to arise, and return to their Father. They have undertaken to return to Christian fundamentals, though the position to which one returns can never be quite the position from which one fell away.

Eliot's poetry shows a steady progression toward religious belief. It is the tortuous progress of the modern intellectual man who recognizes the necessity of religion, but for whom a spontaneous, simple faith is difficult, if not impossible. The poems are an honest record. There are no easy affirmations. What the poems give, instead, is something more valuable: a dramatic and symbolical description of the complex consciousness of a modern intellectual mind.

"The Love Song of J. Alfred Prufrock" is a picture of ineffectualness. Prufrock's condition is symbolized by the comparison between the evening and a patient etherized upon a table. His condition is one of distress and restlessness (for the patient under ether is not really quiet, but infinitely restless) and, at the same time, of paralysis. He is unable to answer questions, either great or small, or to arrive at a decision. He is incapable of action. He is bored by the petty round of tea parties and social calls. He lacks motivation because he is without conviction or belief. Contrasts are suggested with heroic figures of the past: with Hamlet, who, though greatly perturbed by the task thrust upon him, was nevertheless a passionate, heroic figure; with Michelangelo, who epitomizes the creative energy of the Italian Renaissance; with John the Baptist, the first Christian martyr. The presence of allusions like these gives the poem a religious implication: Hamlet, Michelangelo, and John the Baptist were energized by a passionate belief; Prufrock is separated from them by the distance between health and neurosis.

The ironic futility of "Prufrock" is continued in *The Waste Land,* but the despair is greater, and the religious implications correspondingly more emphatic. It is as if the poet meant to suggest that man must be reduced to utter despair before there can be a conscious striving toward religious faith, that God's opportunity must wait upon

man's extremity. Many passages in *The Waste Land* point
to a religious interpretation. The desert passages recall the
Old Testament in both tone and language. Eliot's "Son of
man,/ You cannot say, or guess, for you know only/
A heap of broken images" is reminiscent of Ezekiel's "Son
of man, can these bones live? And I answered, O Lord God,
thou knowest." Ecclesiastes, Chapter 12, describes a waste
land similar to Eliot's: ". . . and the grasshopper shall be
a burden, and desire shall fail . . ." The allusion to
Christ's agony and death ("After the torchlight red on
sweaty faces/ After the frosty silence in the garden/ After
the agony. . . .") suggests the Christian solution.

Ash Wednesday is perhaps the chief Christian poem of
our time. It describes the progress of the soul from despair
to hope, from unbelief to belief. The hopelessness of the
opening lines seems as profound as that of *The Waste
Land,* and more apathetic:

> Because I do not hope to turn again
> Because I do not hope
> Because I do not hope to turn . . .
> Because I do not hope to know again
> The infirm glory of the positive hour
> Because I do not think
> Because I know I shall not know. . . .

Prufrock's uncertainty was not greater than that of the
"I" of these lines. But the ending is very different from
Prufrock's. Prufrock ended with a sensation of drowning;
his inadequacy is such that he is overwhelmed by the demands of life. *Ash Wednesday* ends with a prayer which is
not the soliloquy of a beholding and jubilant soul, but a
petition for grace to subject the individual will to the divine will:

> Teach us to care and not to care
> Teach us to sit still

> Even among these rocks,
> Our peace in His will. . . .

"Teach us to care and not to care" well expresses the central Christian paradox, the apparent contradiction between individual responsibility and divine sovereignty. The Christian faith posits the active, responsible, even militant individual, the individual who has put on the whole armor of God, ready to do battle against principalities and powers and the rulers of darkness. This is an individual who "cares" intensely. Over against this is set reliance upon, and submission to, an overruling Providence. The two concepts operate on entirely different "levels." One concept counsels vigilance, effort; the other, faith, submission.

Between *Ash Wednesday* and *Four Quartets* Eliot developed in the direction of a more philosophic religious attitude. *Four Quartets* is a series of religious meditations. The series reaches its culmination in "Little Gidding," which takes its name from a famous Anglican shrine in Huntingdonshire, where Nicholas Ferrar and his family, in 1625, retired to lead a life of religious devotion, and where Charles I, "a broken king," came to pray. It is a place, the poem says, "where prayer has been valid." The protagonist of the poem visits Little Gidding to pray, or at least to assume the attitude of prayer: "You are here to kneel." But true prayer is not easy, for "prayer is more/ Than an order of words, the conscious occupation/ Of the praying mind, or the sound of the voice praying." The modern intellectual man is different from the seventeenth-century worshippers at Little Gidding. To the modern intellectual visitor, even with the best of intentions, this shrine, or any other shrine, is likely to be only "a shell, a husk of meaning."

Man is capable of moments of illumination when the timeless touches or intersects the temporal ("the intersec-

tion of the timeless moment," "this intersection time").
The meeting with the "dead master" during the bombing
of London is such a moment. Experience, the poem seems
to say, is a preparation for the "intersection time," the moment of insight or revelation. The preparation is a purification by fire. Fire, indeed, seems the dominant symbol
of the poem. In Part 1, the sun shines with "pentecostal
fire." In Part 2, fire appears as "the flickering tongue" of
a bomber, shockingly contrasted with the "cloven tongues"
of Pentecost. Part 4 repeats the fire motif, particularly in
"the intolerable shirt of flame," the Nessus shirt of Hercules. But in whatever manifestation, the fire is for man's
behoof; it is "refining" (this is the lesson of the dead master); it is "devised" by "Love."

More than any other twentieth-century poet writing
in English, Eliot takes us into the heart of the devotional,
the liturgical, the sacramental aspects of Christianity. Many
of his poems can be regarded as prayers and liturgies. The
liturgical tone is often definitely suggested by quoted
phrases from the Anglican or Catholic service, as, for example, by these lines in *Ash Wednesday* from the "Hail
Mary": "Pray for us sinners now and at the hour of our
death,/ Pray for us now and at the hour of our death."

To Eliot the Christian faith and worship are a discipline,
in the practice of which, forms and ceremonies are important, even necessary aids. In "The Dry Salvages," he
speaks of "hints and guesses," by which he means the imperfect insights to which we as human beings are limited,
and then goes on to say, "The rest is prayer, observance,
discipline, thought, and action." Always Eliot's emphasis
is upon the disciplined personality. In his "Thoughts After
Lambeth," he says that Christianity is "difficult both to the
disorderly mind and to the unruly passions." And always
Eliot is concerned with the great question of salvation.
"Where shall the word be found?" he asks repeatedly, re-
ferring back to St. John's "In the beginning was the word."

If *Ash Wednesday* (1930) is perhaps the outstanding explicitly Christian poem of our century, *Death Comes for the Archbishop* (1927) is perhaps the outstanding explicitly Christian novel. Eliot belongs to that branch of the Anglican Church which would like to see the ancient breach with Rome healed, while at the same time finding certain Roman doctrines—papal infallibility is one—an obstacle. Willa Cather, though not technically a convert to Rome, could hardly have written of Catholicism with greater warmth and sympathy had she been one. Her novel is the inspiring story of the missionary labors of two Catholic priests in the old Spanish Southwest. These labors culminated in the building of the Cathedral in Sante Fe. "Where there is great love," Father Latour said, "there are always miracles. The miracles of the Church seem to me to rest not so much upon faces or voices or healing power coming suddenly near to us from afar off, but upon our perceptions being made finer, so that for a moment our eyes can see and our ears can hear what there is about us always." A Catholic commentator has spoken of what he calls "Miss Cather's perfect assimilation of Catholic usage" in *Death Comes For the Archbishop*.

It is not easy to say how influential the religious examples of Eliot and Cather have been upon American writers, or how prognostic their religious histories may be of future trends in our literature. One has the feeling that the religious trend in literature is becoming more marked, without at the moment being able to offer a large documentation. The conversion of Allen Tate to Rome is worthy of mention, especially since Catholicism has not been known to flourish particularly in his part of the South—Kentucky-Tennessee. Readers of his future works will probably be on the lookout for evidence of Catholic influence. John Henry Newman, who more than a century ago traveled the churchly road from Oxford to Rome, declared in his *Apologia* that "there is no medium, in true philosophy, between Atheism and Catholicity, and a perfectly consistent mind, under those circumstances in which it finds itself here below, must embrace either the one or the other." The Cardinal's dictum is of course unacceptable to the great world of Protestantism, but it has the merit, at least, of pointing to the dissatisfaction which the seeker after belief, today, is likely to feel, more and more, in various sorts of "middle ground."

The virtue of ritualistic discipline (so much emphasized in the Anglican and Catholic Churches), which appealed to Eliot and Willa Cather, has been made much of by some writers whom one might hesitate to designate, technically, as Christians. I have in mind, particularly, Ernest Hemingway, of whom Carlos Baker has said, "The consciousness of God is in his books, and the Book of Common Prayer is seldom far out of his reach." The ritualistic aspect is seen throughout Hemingway, but best perhaps in some of his shorter pieces. One might almost substitute "sacramental" for "ritualistic," remembering the "Catechism" of the *Book of Common Prayer,* where "sacrament" is defined as "an outward and visible sign of an inward and spiritual grace."

"A Clean, Well-Lighted Place" tells about a café and two waiters, and an elderly customer who stays on after all the other customers have left, drinking his brandy meticulously and deliberately. The elderly gentleman is there every night, and he is obviously reluctant to leave this clean, well-lighted place. Past eighty, he must have been a rather special person in former years (he still is): his strong head for brandy (a liquor for heroes, Dr. Johnson said [2]), his ability, though a little drunk, to drink without spilling, and at last to walk away "with dignity," though a bit unsteadily—these connote a certain distinction of character. Care and precision mark the manner in which the

---

[2] "Claret is the liquor for boys, port for men; but he who aspires to be a hero, must drink brandy." (Boswell's *Life of Johnson*)

waiter serves his customer: "He put down the saucer and poured the glass full of brandy. . . . The old man motioned with his finger. 'A little more,' he said. The waiter poured on into the glass so that the brandy slopped over and ran down the stem into the top saucer of the pile." One can be sure that in the first instance the glass was filled in exactly the right amount, and in the second, the excess was exactly measured, also. Bartenders (a favorite symbolic character in Hemingway) are careful and precise. They are, in the present story, ministering priests, as it were, at this ritual.

The café becomes a symbol, too. It is a lighted area surrounded by darkness. The lighted area seems pitifully small in comparison with the enveloping darkness. If the darkness stands for the disorder and chaos of an evil world, and the spot of light for the small amount of order and discipline and civilization which the individual has been able to wrest out of the surrounding chaos and old night, then, the story seems to say, the small lighted area is enough, or, at any rate, must be made to do. Not to be overlooked, also, is the advantage of human sympathy. The café is a place where congenial souls may meet. The older waiter, particularly, has a sympathetic understanding of the elderly gentleman's problem. Living in a clean, well-lighted place does not mean solitary withdrawal so long as there are others who also prefer such a place. One can belong to a communion of saints, however small.

In "Big Two-Hearted River," the feeling of ritual is even more emphasized. The story gives an account of Nick Adams' fishing expedition in the Michigan woods. We are told of his hike with a heavy pack after leaving the train (one recalls Christian's burden in *Pilgrim's Progress*), the selection of the campsite, pitching tent, cooking the evening meal, the night's sleep, the fishing next day, the throwing back into the water of the trout too small to keep, the avoidance of a place farther downstream which presents special difficulties, and which Nick is not yet spiritually prepared to enter. The whole account has a ceremonial air. It is not a novitiate, for Nick has been there before. But further trial and cleansing are necessary before Nick can fish in the most hazardous waters.

"Big Two-Hearted River" is a religious symbolism. It tells of purgation and preparation. When Nick Adams goes into the woods, he is a sick soul. The spiritual therapy is not the old romantic communing with Nature. (A fisherman's "nature" is different from a romantic poet's.) There is, on the contrary, an exacting procedure which Nick must follow, a course of action which calls out his own powers. Eliot's line quoted above—"The rest is prayer, observance, discipline, thought, and action"—is, interestingly enough, rather applicable to Nick's conduct in "Big Two-Hearted River." The story becomes, at last, a symbol of sacramental living.

It is an easy and inviting transition from Nick Adams of Hemingway's "Big Two-Hearted River" to Ike McCaslin of Faulkner's "The Bear." Both stories have to do with boys who undergo a certain spiritual preparation, and both stories have the aura of ritual and sacrament.[3] One difference worth noting is that Nick goes on his expedition alone, while Ike goes in the company of his elders. Nick is on his own; Ike is a learner. But both, it should be observed, are following a traditional procedure, a long established ritual. It would be a mistake, I think, to infer from Nick's aloneness that he is not part of a traditional society. He has learned from his father before him. Fishermen as well as hunters belong to a noble company. But it is also true that the social and traditional aspects are more prominent in Faulkner's story than in Hemingway's, and this

[3] It would be interesting and perhaps fruitful to compare Eliot, Hemingway, and Faulkner in this matter of ritualistic observance. All three might be discovered to possess the essential quality about equally, the difference being that Eliot is explicitly ecclesiastical and liturgical, while the others are not.

greater prominence would perhaps justify the inference that a stable, traditional society is more important to Faulkner than to Hemingway.

Faulkner glorifies the old hunters. Their talk was "the best of all talking." Sam Fathers, the son of a Negro slave and a Chickasaw chief, was the boy's principal mentor, though he learned, too, from Boon Hogganbeck (who was also part Indian), from the educated leaders—Major de Spain, General Compson, and cousin McCaslin—from Ash, the Negro cook, and even from Tennie's Jim. The animals, also, were his instructors—the lesser ones as well as Old Ben and Lion. In such a school, the boy learned humility and patience and the conquest of fear. Fathers told the boy, "Be scared. You can't help that. But don't be afraid. Ain't nothing in the woods going to hurt you if you don't corner it, or it don't smell that you are afraid." The crowning spiritual grace was a kind of surrender, which was achieved when the boy, his novitiate completed, entered the forest alone, and without gun, watch, or compass.

(Here then—to recur to the earlier comparison—Ike was alone after all, like Nick. Perhaps Nick's aloneness was preceded by a social preparation; perhaps the kind of healing Nick was seeking was something which one can win only by oneself. In any case, the two stories encompass both the social and the individual phases, and seem to say that the very last steps to salvation must be taken alone.)

Faulkner's hunting world is a world of noble qualities. The men observe a long-established ritual. It is a society where every man has his place and knows it, where rank is respected, and merit too, where rank is likely to have a solid basis in merit, and where the idea of responsibility, of *noblesse oblige,* is operative. The boy's attitude toward this society of hunters is one of respect and admiration, and he feels great satisfaction in their recognition of his worthiness.

The contrast between the hunting story (in Parts 1, 2,

and 3) and the story of the "old ledgers" in Part 4 (which gives the history of the McCaslin family from Ike's grandfather down), is a shocking one, for one story is heroic, and the other sordid. The sordidness derives chiefly from the evils of slavery. The plantation economy, Faulkner emphasizes, was founded upon injustice, the injustice of Negro slavery. "This whole land, the whole South," Ike McCaslin cries out, and the author seems to be crying out with him, "is cursed, and all of us who derive from it, whom it ever suckled, white and black both, lie under the curse."

If one asks which story is true, the heroic one of the hunters, or the sordid one of the dealers in slaves, the answer must be that both are true. Man is both sordid and heroic. Man—as Captain Peleg said of Captain Ahab—is both ungodly and Godlike. The special advantage of Faulkner's technique, by which he combines two stories into one, is that he can in this way suggest the fundamental ambiguity, the basic duality, of man's nature. Man is the child of God, made a little lower than the angels. He is also fallen man, born in sin and conceived in iniquity. Both sides are intensified in Faulkner, elevated to high tragedy. The tragedy of man grows out of the conflict between the high impulses and the low, grows out of the coexistence of potentialities for good and for evil. Faulkner likes to juxtapose, shockingly, the two potentialities. Hawthorne (whom Faulkner resembles in many ways [4]) juxtaposed them effectively in the portrait of Arthur Dimmesdale.

The particular symbolisms in "The Bear" are probably best left to the individual reader. Faulkner's great hunt recalls Melville's, but with important differences as well as similarities. The Bear, like the Whale, takes on a mythical, supernatural quality. But the Bear, unlike the Whale,

[4] The reader is referred to a brief elaboration of the resemblance in an article by the present writer, "Hawthorne and Faulkner," *College English* (February, 1956), and a fuller treatment by William Van O'Connor, "Hawthorne and Faulkner: Some Common Ground," *Virginia Quarterly Review* (Winter, 1957).

seems more benign than sinister, and the hunt of the Bear, unlike the hunt of the Whale, is conducted reverently, not blasphemously. The aid called in, in the hunt of the Whale is the Devil's agent, Fedallah; the aid, and an effective aid he proves to be, in the hunt of the Bear is the dog Lion. It may be stretching a point to suggest that Lion is symbolically "the Lion of the tribe of Judah" of the Book of Revelation. But it is not too much to say that Ahab is Devil-inspired in his quest, and Ike and his associates are God-inspired. There is an aura of piety (in the best, older sense) in "The Bear" which is absent from *Moby Dick.*

The Lion of Judah I take to be a type of Christ, and the point recalls Faulkner's fondness for the Christ-symbol. He likes to create characters who resemble Christ, not at all in their totality, but in a few particulars. One such character is Benjy in *The Sound and the Fury,* who recalls Christ in his innocence and his sorrowfulness. Benjy's sorrowful wail seems nothing less than a lament over a lost world; he seems the Spirit itself making intercession for us with groanings which cannot be uttered. Another is Joe Christmas, in *Light in August,* who is a kind of scapegoat, on whose head have been heaped all the sins since the race began, and who suffers a bitter agony, and death at last, at the hands of "soldiers" not unlike those who crucified Christ. Ike McCaslin in *The Bear* is another, who after his long novitiate, renounced his landed inheritance (tainted as it was with the curse of slavery), and took up the carpenter's trade, "because," he said, "if the Nazarene had found carpentering good for the life and ends He had assumed and elected to serve, it would be all right, too, for Isaac McCaslin." And still another is the Corporal, in *A Fable,* whose history parallels Christ's at several points. Faulkner is definitely fascinated by this kind of symbolism. The effect is at least threefold: first, the reader is shocked by the recognition of similarities to Christ in a character who, in other respects, is so un-Christlike; second, the character is deepened and enriched by this added dimension; and third, the idea is conveyed, gradually and firmly, that Christian meanings can have a surprising ubiquity.

Faulkner is still, I fear, a much misunderstood author. He is still read by some as a sociologist. But he is not a sociologist at all. He is, rather, a great imaginative, symbolical writer, a moral allegorist. We do not read Faulkner to learn about Mississippi in a sociological sense, anymore than we read Hawthorne to learn about Massachusetts, or Melville to learn about maritime practices, or Shakespeare to discover economic and social conditions in sixteenth-century England. Let not the Mississippians suppose that Faulkner is writing about them in an exclusive sense, and let not the New Englanders or the Middle Westerners or the Californians, even, suppose that he is *not* writing about them, because he is. Faulkner is not reporting on "conditions"; he is reporting on the human condition. He is reporting on Original Sin, which is—there are good reasons to believe—in widest commonalty spread.

Faulkner is an elemental writer, like Melville and Shakespeare. He writes in his own powerful idiom; he is not concerned with surface pleasantries; he is not a "polite" author; he is concerned with profundities; he is concerned with the soul of man laid bare. To the prudish objection which one critic has made to *The Sound and the Fury,* that it is "about ugly people in an ugly land," the answer might well be, So is *King Lear. The London Times Literary Supplement* (in that historic number devoted to American writing today [5]) had this to say about Faulkner: "Faulkner is all true —he is poetically the most accurate man alive; he has looked straight into the heart of the matter, and got it down for good." The matter which he has looked straight into the heart of, we may be sure, is not peculiar to Mississippi. It is peculiar only to the human race.

Faulkner said in the Stockholm speech, "I believe that

[5] September 17, 1954.

man will prevail." A writer for one of the magazines professed to be puzzled by the word *prevail*, and decided that
it is vague and meaningless. I would suggest, however, that
it might be helpful to look up the word in Cruden's *Concordance* to the Bible, and then read the passages (there
are sixty-five) in which it occurs. In general, *prevail* occurs
in contexts where a victory is won with God's help. *Prevail*, as Faulkner uses it, has nothing to do with modern
technology. It is a Biblical word, and has a religious connotation.

Prevailing in Faulkner is never an easy matter. The
Christian view has never underestimated human tribula-
tion. "Nobody knows the trouble I've seen, nobody knows
but Jesus," is the old spiritual's way of saying that suffering has a central and necessary place in Christian doctrine.
Well, Faulkner's protagonists are nearly always up to their
ears in trouble, are nearly always surrounded by hell and
high water. They may find release only in a martyr's death.
But they always tower. They always enhance our concep-
tion of the human potential.

Faulkner's most heroic character is his most Christian
character: "Dilsey closed the door and returned to the
kitchen. The stove was almost cold. Ise seed de first en de
last, she said, looking at the cold stove, Ise seed de first en
de last. She set out some cold food on the table. As she
moved back and forth, she sang a hymn. She sang the first
two lines over and over to the complete tune." Above the
ruins of the House of Compson, Dilsey, the old Negro servant, towers. Dilsey's towering strength is founded on Christian faith. It is a rugged faith, from which she refuses to be
separated by death, or life, or angels, or principalities, or
powers, or things present, or things to come, or height, or
depth, or any other creature.

Faulkner embodies and dramatizes the basic Christian
concepts so effectively that he can with justice be regarded
as one of the most profoundly Christian writers in our

time. There is everywhere in his writings the basic premise of Original Sin; everywhere the conflict between the flesh and the spirit. One finds also the necessity of discipline, of trial by fire in the furnace of affliction, of sacrifice and the sacrificial death, of redemption through sacrifice. Man in Faulkner is a heroic, tragic figure. He may on occasion rise to spiritual greatness. The greatness is measured by the distance between the heights he attains and the depths to which he descends, or, but for the grace of God, might have descended.

Robert Penn Warren's fiction resembles Faulkner's in several ways—in a vigorous handling of Southern subject matter, in a philosophical and religious position rooted in Southern tradition, in technical virtuosity, in symbolical intensity. Warren's work, too, (again like Faulkner's) is infused with a kind of neo-Calvinism. But Warren is no mere disciple. He strikes out on his own.

In *All the King's Men,* Boss Willie Stark, "the man of fact," explains to Dr. Adam Stanton, "the man of idea," that there is no such thing as natural goodness, and goes on to give his pragmatic version of how "good" and "bad" jostle each other in this imperfect world:

"Yeah," the Boss said, "he was one of those guys wants everything and wants everything two ways at once. You know the kind, Doc?"

He flicked a look over at Adam, like a man flicking a fly over by the willows in the trout stream. But there wasn't any strike.

"Yeah, old Hugh—he never learned that you can't have everything. That you can have mighty little. And you never have anything you don't make. Just because he inherited a little money and the name Miller, he thought you could have everything. Yeah, and he wanted the one last damned thing you can't inherit. And you know what it is?" He stared at Adam's face.

"What?" Adam said, after a long pause.

"Goodness. Yeah, just plain, simple goodness. Well, you can't inherit that from anybody. You got to make it, Doc. If you want it. And you got to make it out of badness. Badness. And you know why, Doc?" He raised his bulk up in the broken-down wreck of an overstuffed chair he was in, and leaned forward, his hands on his knees, his elbows cocked out, his head outthrust and the hair coming down to his eyes, and stared into Adam's face. "Out of badness," he repeated. "And you know why? Because there isn't anything else to make it out of."

The passage is a down-to-earth statement of Original Sin. Not natural goodness but natural badness is what we have to work with.

Human nature is corrupt and corruptible. Percy Munn, in *Night Rider,* is one of Warren's more memorable characters. A tobacco raiser and country-town lawyer, educated in Philadelphia and highly respected in his community, Munn is a kind of modern Southern Brutus, an honorable man who is seduced by conspirators or organizers who are also honorable men for the most part, and who set out quite honorably and justifiably to redress a great wrong, namely, the cheating of the tobacco growers by the Tobacco Trust. But the conspirators go down hill, and Munn goes down hill with them. He joins the night riders. He sets fire to barns; he commits murder; he becomes bestial sexually. Natural badness is triumphant. And there is an inexorableness (reminding one of Hawthorne) about it all. Having taken the first step almost involuntarily, Munn goes inevitably, step by step, to his doom.

Warren's "Original Sin: A Short Story" (it is a short poem) gives another (quite different) account of a lost innocence. If *Night Rider* shows a man, Percy Munn, sinking into a depravity which is astonishing to those who behold him, and most of all perhaps to Munn himself, "Original Sin: A Short Story" shows, through symbolic images, a process of growth and maturation (ostensibly an "upward" rather than a "downward" course), in which there is involved necessarily an unhappy conflict between the new and the old, maturity and childhood, experience and innocence. The narrator's country boyhood (suggested by such images as "the old hound that used to snuffle your door and moan," "an old horse cold in the pasture") is contrasted with an intellectually distinguished maturity (suggested by such images as "Harvard Yard," "the quantum glare of the sun"). The narrator is haunted by childhood ghosts, which he equates with a lost innocence. Perhaps the narrator, somewhat in the manner of Hawthorne's Ethan Brand, left the simple life of his youth behind in quest of some high abstraction. He cries, "There must be a new innocence for us to be stayed by." It is the cry everywhere of the modern intellectual man. Where is this new innocence? Where shall the word be found?

Warren's book-length poem, *Brother to Dragons,* which has been used in an earlier connection, contains some fairly explicit statements which perhaps can be regarded as giving an "answer," or a part of an answer, to questions like these. The poem is one of the most impressive treatments in modern American literature of the problem presented by the human condition.

The human condition, in the first place, is (as we study its dramatizations in the poem) one of extremity. There can be no hope so long as the recognition of this basic fact is absent. It is to a realization of man's extremity that Jefferson, in this posthumous inquiry, has come painfully and by degrees. Man learns only through suffering. Near the end of the poem, a changed Jefferson speaks:

Now I should hope to find the courage to say
That the dream of the future is not
Better than the fact of the past, no matter how terrible.
For without the fact of the past we cannot dream the future.
I think I begin to see the forging of the future.
It will be forged beneath the hammer of truth
On the anvil of anguish. We shall be forged
Beneath the hammer of truth on the anvil of anguish.

And Jefferson's sister, Lucy, says:

But my dear Brother, if your dream
Was noble, there's a nobler yet to dream.
It will be nobler because more difficult and cold
In the face of the old cost of the human redemption,
And the knowledge of that cost is in itself a kind of redemption.

"The old cost of the human redemption!" That, of course, is the great Christian thesis: man's need of redemption, and its great cost.

The human condition, secondly, is one of paradox. Paradox is at the heart of Christian doctrine. "He that is greatest among you shall be your servant." "Many that are first shall be last; and the last shall be first." "Whosoever will save his life shall lose it; but whosoever will lose his life for my sake, the same shall save it." In the last speech of the poem the author attempts to sum up in a series of paradoxes the wisdom, the Christian wisdom, which the poem has wrung out of this tragic tale:

The recognition of complicity is the beginning of innocence,
The recognition of necessity is the beginning of freedom,
The recognition of the direction of fulfillment is the death of
    the self,
And the death of the self is the beginning of selfhood.

The human condition, imperfect and predestined in the high religious sense as it is, is, once more, a condition of responsibility. The idea of responsibility is included, indeed, in the word "complicity" in the passage just quoted; we are all, in a profound sense, accomplices, and complicity is inevitable. At the very end of *Brother to Dragons*, the author visited the grave of Jefferson's nephew, Lilburn Lewis, the murderer. "Why am I here?" he asks, and answers, "Some need has drawn me." And then, in the poem's last lines, the author says,

And so I stood on the headland and stared at the river,
In the last light of December's, and the day's declension.

And the river declared its cold gleam beyond the flat land . . .
I went down the bluff, and crossed the evening barnlot,
I opened the sagging gate, and was prepared
To go into the world of action and liability.

The last word in the quotation, *liability*, should be noted especially. "Liable" has two complementary meanings: (1) obligated by or answerable to law (as in "liable for military service"), and (2) exposed to danger or risk (as in "liable to err"). "Liability" is, therefore, a particularly happy word choice, for it comprises two paradoxical aspects of the human condition: man's responsibility and his fallibility. Christian doctrine insists to the last that man is fallible *and* responsible, that he is responsible though fallen.

* *Conclusion*

IN A TV ADVERTISEMENT, a man drives his car into a quick-wash place, rolls up his windows, and while the water pours around him, plugs in his electric razor, and shaves himself. As he drives out he lowers the window, and sticking out his head, announces ecstatically to his audience, "It's a *wonderful world* when a man can have a car-wash and shave all in one minute!" (O brave new world, that has such gadgets in it!)

A distinguished speaker at a national political convention declared that we are the finest nation in the world, and went on to express the hope that we would "continue to deserve God's blessings." (A familiar Christian prayer reminds us that "we do not trust in our own righteousness, but in God's manifold and great mercies.")

One rubs one's eyes and ears incredulously in encountering such attitudes, and they are, I fear, representative. One wonders to what low levels our culture may not sink. For nothing can be more anti-Christian than the materialism of the first illustration, or the self-righteousness of the second. If most people (as seems likely) are unaware of an absurdity in either instance, why then, that fact only makes the situation all the worse.

One wonders, too, to what extent such materialism and such self-righteousness may be a part of our alleged "tradition," and to what extent some of our most celebrated writers, whether wittingly or unwittingly, may have helped shape such a "tradition." And one fears that some of them have much to answer for.

147

I have tried to distinguish three views of man which I take to be erroneous, when judged by Christian standards, whether Protestant or Catholic.[1]

One is the error of the rationalists, who advised man to rely exclusively upon his own unaided reason. "Fix reason firmly in her seat, and call to her tribunal every fact, every opinion. . . . Your own reason is the only oracle given you by heaven," said Jefferson. If man would rely exclusively upon his reason, the rationalists thought, all would be well. But there were two things wrong with this: (1) man, in spite of everything, often behaves irrationally; and (2) reason alone, even if man were capable of complete rationality at all times, is not enough to satisfy man's spiritual needs.

A second error was the romantic deification of man, as proclaimed by Emerson and Whitman. The error here lies both in the denial of Original Sin and in the failure to distinguish between Creator and Creature. Man is confused with God, to the long-run detriment of man. For the long-run result was a fatal pride, an exaggerated individualism.

The third erroneous view which I have tried to define is found in the premises of the modern naturalistic novel. Here man becomes the mechanical product of the forces of heredity and environment—of environment, especially. He ceases to be a moral agent. The Christian emphasis on a spiritual rebirth ("Ye must be born again!") is supplanted by an emphasis on the improvement of "conditions." Although it is too early to estimate the eventual influence of this view, it has already had a strong impact on the popular mind.

On the other side, the Christian side, writers of the nine-

[1] If I seem to have neglected Catholic literature in this study, the reason is the obvious one that, until very recently, there has been a dearth of Catholic writers in our literature. Our imaginative writers of stature, with few exceptions, have had their being within the framework of the Protestant tradition.

148

teenth century like Hawthorne, Melville, and James were not satisfied with the prevailing romanticism, which inflated the individual. Hawthorne's stories illustrated the perils of "self-trust." Melville showed the catastrophic end of an irresponsible, devil-inspired individual. James dramatized the miseries of the overcultivated Ego.

And on the Christian side also, writers of our own century like Cather, Eliot, Faulkner, and Warren have been dissatisfied with the prevailing naturalism, which relieves man of responsibility and reduces him to an amoral puppet. They have taken the Christian view that man is a battleground. For man embodies both good and evil. God and the Devil are still active in the world, and man's spiritual victories are won with God's help, and in Hell's despite. That is what Faulkner means by man's "prevailing."

Man is a moral agent, and a tragic figure. The tragic aspect is brought out with special power in Hawthorne, Melville, and Faulkner. Dimmesdale confessing on the scaffold, Ahab blaspheming as he makes his last suicidal attack on the Whale, Joe Christmas hounded to his death and mutilated by a Yoknapatawpha Centurion—these are characters and situations that illustrate the eternal moral warfare which makes man the tragic figure that he is.

For man is an imperfect, nonperfectible being. He cannot be improved by technology. He is not a machine, but a very fallible human. Poor wayward creature, he appears even now to be plotting, with all ingenuity and speed, his own destruction. But his state, unless by his own perverse wilfulness, is not beyond the reach of God's redeeming grace. This is the essence of the human condition, and the Christian hope. And this is the meaning of the dramatizations of human experience by the greatest American writers.

✳ *Index*

Adams, Henry, 26
Adams, John Quincy, 59
Addison, Joseph, 23–24
Age of Reason, The, 24, 26–28
Aldridge, John W., 118 n
All the King's Men, 142–43
Ambassadors, The, 17–18, 103, 104
American Renaissance, 16
"American Scholar, The," 44
American Tragedy, An, 113, 114–19, 124; compared with *The Sound and the Fury,* 119; with *The Scarlet Letter,* 120; with *Huckleberry Finn,* 121
Anderson, Sherwood, 119
Andrewes, Lancelot, 8
Apologia Pro Vita Sua, 133–34
Arminianism, compared with Calvinism, 12–13
Arnold, Matthew, 6, 18, 126
Arrowsmith, 122
"Ash Wednesday," 130–31, 132

"Bacchus," 70
Baker, Carlos, 134
"Ballad of Trees and the Master, A," 67, 72
Baptists, the, debates with the Methodists, 12
Bear, The, 136–39; compared with *Moby Dick,* 97–98, 138–39; with "Big, Two-Hearted River," 136–37
"Beast in the Jungle, The," 104–106
Bentham, Jeremy, 49

Bible, the, stylistic influence of, 3; Paine's rejection of, 26–28; Jefferson's view of, 29; Channing's view of, 35; Emerson's view of, 51–53; allusions to: Deuteronomy, 86; Psalms, 24, 28, 111–12; Ecclesiastes, 130; Ezekiel, 130; Jonah, 97; Matthew, 80, 84; Mark, 78; Luke, 71; John, 63, 132; Acts, 34; Paul's Epistles, 7, 54, 59, 83, 100, 108, 122–23; Revelation, 139
"Big Two-Hearted River," 135–37; compared with *The Bear,* 136–37
Billy Budd, 98–102; compared with "The Birthmark," 98–100; Billy as Christ-symbol, 100, 101, 102
"Birthmark, The," 16, 79–81; compared with *Billy Budd,* 98–100; with *The Portrait of a Lady,* 104
Bloudy Tenent of Persecution for Cause of Conscience, The, 5
Book of Common Prayer, The, 56, 134
"Boston Hymn, The," 127 n
Boswell, James, 134 n
Bradford, William, 3
Bradley, A. C., 101
Brontë, Charlotte, 71
Brooks, Van Wyck, 50–51
Brother to Dragons, 40–42, 144–46
Bryant, William Cullen, 39, 45
Burke, Edmund, 5, 25
Burns, Robert, 44

Calvin, John, 12

Harvard University, 36, 37, 46, 53, 144
Hathorne, John, 16
Hathorne, William, 16
Hawthorne, Mrs. Nathaniel, 76
Hawthorne, Nathaniel, 4, 15–18 *passim*, 20, 28, 45, 51, 53–54, 59, 69, 70, 71, 73, 74, 75–89, 106, 125, 127, 138, 140, 143, 144, 149; friendship with Melville, 75–79
"Hawthorne and his Mosses," 75–76, 94
"He preached upon breadth," 128
"Hebraism and Hellenism," 6–7, 18–19
Hemingway, Ernest, 120 n, 123, 134–37; not a naturalist, 123; compared with Eliot and Faulkner, 136 n
Hercules, 132
History of Plymouth Plantation, 4
Hitler, Adolf, 91
Holmes, Oliver Wendell, 53
Horses and Men, 119
House of the Seven Gables, The, 77
Howells, William Dean, 35
Huckleberry Finn, 120–21
Hulme, T. E., 46

I'll Take My Stand, 5
In Memoriam, 30
In Our Time, 120 n
Institutes of Christianity, 12
Irving, Washington, 39

Jackson, Andrew, 59
Jackson, Thomas Jonathan (Stonewall), 20
James, Henry, 15–19 *passim*, 73, 102–106, 149
Jefferson, Thomas, 5, 23, 24, 28–30, 39–40, 41, 42, 144–45, 148
Jesus, the view of held by Franklin, 32–33; by Emerson, 49–50; the treatment of by Lanier, 67, 68, 72; by Dickinson, 71–72; Christ-symbols, 100, 101, 102, 139–40
John the Baptist, 129
Johnson, Samuel, 134
Journal to Stella, The, 25

Journals, The (of Emerson), 74
Jungle, The, 121–22

Kant, Immanuel, 38, 49
Keats, John, 44
King, Miles, 31
King Lear, compared with *The Sound and the Fury*, 140
Knickerbocker History of New York, 39

Lanier, Sidney, 44, 65–69, 72
Laud, Archbishop William, 5
Leaves of Grass, 60–65, 75
Lee, Robert E., 21
"Lee in the Mountains," 21
Lewis, Meriwether, 41–42
Lewis, Sinclair, 122–23
Liberalism, characteristics of, 126–28
Life of Johnson, 134 n
Light in August, 139, 149
"Little Gidding," 17, 131–32
Locke, John, 10
Longfellow, Henry Wadsworth, 53
"Love Song of J. Alfred Prufrock, The," 18, 129, 130
Lowell, James Russell, 53
Luther, Martin, 36

McTeague, 112
Maggie, A Girl of the Streets, 109, 112
Main Currents in American Thought, 39
Main Street, 122–23
Marble Faun, The, 82
Marlowe, Christopher, 97
Marquand, John P., 35
"Marshes of Glynn, The," 44, 66–69
Mather, Cotton, 8
Matthiessen, F. O., 16
"Maypole of Merrymount, The," 4
Melville, Herman, 20, 28, 51, 73–74, 89–102, 106, 125, 138–39, 140, 149; friendship with Hawthorne, 75–79
Mencken, H. L., 4, 16, 18
Methodists, the, debates with the Baptists, 12
Michelangelo, 129

153